CONTENTS

INTRODUCTION

The *Basic Guide to Dressmaking* has been written for fashion enthusiasts who have often been tempted to make their own clothes, but have never had the confidence to make a start. This book will change all that by taking you through the basic skills from start to finish. It begins by explaining how to choose and cut patterns for women, men and children, then helps you to understand putting the garment together from darts, sleeves, yokes and hems to fasteners and finishings.

All the techniques are simply and clearly explained with full-color photographs, step-by-step illustrations and charts to guide you every inch of the way. Each chapter also includes handy tips and hints to help you get the best and most professional-looking results every time.

With this book the absolute beginner can successfully start to make clothes for all the family – or the more experienced dressmaker can find useful advice to add to her existing skills. Whatever your dressmaking requirements, the *Basic Guide to Dressmaking* will teach you the essential techniques so that, before you know it, you will be able to tackle any pattern that appeals to you with all the confidence of a professional.

SEWING GUIDE
Care of a sewing machine

Take care of your sewing machine, and use it correctly, and it will give good service for many years, however often you use it. Keep the machine covered while not in use to protect it from dust. If it is kept in a cold part of the house, bring it out a few hours before you intend to use it so that it reaches room temperature. This is important because the oil on the moving parts needs to be warm in order to lubricate properly.

Choose the correct needle size and type, and the correct thread for the fabric, thread the machine as directed in your machine manual, then switch on. Check the tension, presser foot pressure and stitch length before beginning to stitch the garment itself.

Tension
The machine is set at the correct tension when the knots of the stitches are in the center of the fabric, rather than on the top or bottom. Try out the stitch on scraps of fabric, using a doubled piece or two thicknesses, as most stitching is through two layers. On the same fabric, straight stitching, zigzag and

Left to right: Too much presser foot pressure, too little presser foot pressure and tight top tension.

decorative stitches may all need a different tension and should be checked separately before use. Although you can alter the bobbin thread tension by turning the screw holding the tension spring on the bobbin case, this is rarely done as it is simpler to alter the top thread tension. For either alteration, make only a small turn of the knob or screw, which should be sufficient however bad the tension problem seems. If the knots are in the center of the fabric but the stitching still causes puckering, try shortening the stitch length. With the right needle, thread and stitch length, the tension should need little or no adjustment except when working with bulky or difficult fabrics.

Feed and pressure
The teeth below the presser foot feed the fabric through evenly, and are only lowered or covered for darning. The pressure of the lowered presser foot holds the fabric in place over the fabric feed teeth. On some machines, there is an automatic adjustment of pressure to accommodate finer or bulkier fabrics. On others, this pressure can be adjusted manually. Too much pressure damages the fabric or causes puckering, while too little pressure causes the feed to be uneven or ineffective.

Cleaning
Switch off the machine and remove the needle before cleaning to avoid the danger of accidentally catching your fingers. Most dust and thread collects around the bobbin and under the fabric feed. Dust frequently here, especially when sewing velvet, corduroy and other napped fabrics, using a fine brush. Do not be tempted to take out stray bits of thread with a hard or pointed implement, as it is easy to cause damage. Clean the tension disks with a fine soft cloth, putting the cloth between the disks, lowering the presser foot lever, and pulling the cloth through in the direction in which the thread would move. Clean the thread guide, and needle and presser foot bars. Wipe the surface of the machine occasionally with a cloth dampened with soapy water.

Oiling
Use only sewing machine oil. Oil the points indicated in your sewing machine manual using one or two drops at a time. Always oil the bobbin area after cleaning. A machine used often needs oiling two or three times a year. If it has not been used during the previous two weeks, oil before use. Too much oil leads to oil marks on the fabric, so stitch on spare pieces of fabric after oiling to be sure there is no excess oil. A well-cared-for machine will need servicing once a year at the most. When you do have it serviced, use an authorized dealer for your make of machine.

6

Adjusting the tension

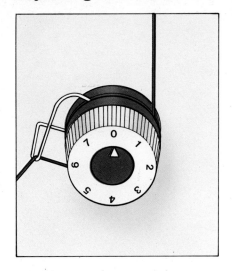

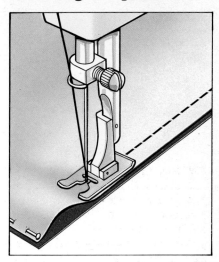

1 *If the knot forms on the top or the stitching is puckered, turn the knob to a lower number or minus sign (−). If the knot forms at the bottom or stitches are loose, turn to a higher number or plus sign (+).*

2 *If the knot forms on the top, turn the screw on the bobbin case clockwise to tighten the bobbin tension. When the knot forms on the bottom, turn the screw counter-clockwise to loosen it. Make small adjustments only and test the stitch on a spare piece of fabric.*

Checking the pressure

Cut two pieces of fabric on the straight grain about 6in long and pin together at each end. Stitch along the grain between pins. If there is more top fabric than bottom fabric on reaching the second pin, reduce the pressure on the presser foot.

Cleaning

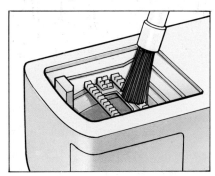

1 *Use a brush to clean around the fabric feed and bobbin casing. Then oil with one drop of oil at the points indicated in the machine manual.*

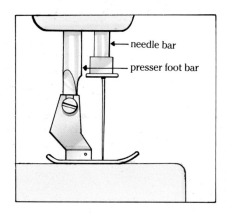

needle bar

presser foot bar

2 *Use a brush on the needle bar, presser foot bar and thread guides. Clean the disks on the tension unit by passing a fine cloth between them.*

HELPING HAND

Identifying stitching problems

• **Needle breaking**
Needle wrong type for machine or fabric
Needle incorrectly inserted
Bent needle
Needle too fine for fabric
Presser foot loose or unsuitable for the stitch
Fabric being pulled through rather than guided and supported

• **Needle thread breaking**
Knotted or uneven thread
Thread too thick for needle
Top of machine incorrectly threaded
Thread not unwinding from the spool
Damaged needle
Needle incorrectly inserted

• **Bobbin thread breaking**
Bobbin too full
Bobbin incorrectly placed in case
Bobbin case incorrectly inserted
Bobbin case (or bobbin) damaged
Bobbin tension too tight
Dust or thread around bobbin case

• **Stitches not forming**
Empty bobbin
Top or bottom of machine threaded incorrectly
Damaged needle
Needle wrong type for machine
Needle wrong size for thread

• **Puckered seam**
Stitch too long
Tension too tight
Thread too thick for fabric
Needle too large for fabric
Damaged needle
Pressure too heavy or light

• **Skipped stitches**
Needle wrong type for fabric
Damaged needle
Thread too thick for needle
Pressure too light
Fabric preventing even feed (use a special purpose presser foot or wash out the finish in the fabric)

• **Noisy or slow machine**
Dust and threads around bobbin casing
Cold machine
Machine needs oiling
Damaged needle
Bobbin winder engaged
Loose flywheel

Stitching by hand

Although a lot of stitching can be done by machine, hand stitches are often better for invisible or especially accurate stitching, and almost every garment will need some hand stitching to catch the facings in position, attach fasteners or finish a hem. A lot of hand stitching can be time consuming, and should not be hurried, so find yourself a comfortable chair with needles, thread, small sharp scissors, pins and pincushion all within easy reach for undisturbed stitching.

Needles

Sharps, betweens and crewel needles are most used in dressmaking. There is a large range of sizes – the higher the number, the finer the needle. The eye of the needle should take the thread without shredding it and the needle should take the thread through the fabric without leaving a permanent hole. A bent, blunt or rusty needle will spoil the stitching, so throw away the imperfect ones immediately. Keep needles in wool flannel to prevent them from rusting.

Sharps are medium length, general purpose needles with round eyes. Use size 7 or 8 for most sewing, and size 9 for sewing silk, chiffon and other fine fabrics. Betweens are similar to sharps but shorter, and are traditionally used for quilting and by professional sewers who find the shorter needle better for quick, even stitching. Crewel needles are used for embroidery and their long eyes make them suitable for use with thicker threads for buttonholes or topstitching by hand.

Other useful needles are ball point needles for knitted and stretch fabrics, glovers' needles, which have triangular points for sewing leather, suede, plastic, vinyl and fur, and straw needles, which are longer than sharps and useful for basting.

Threading a needle

Use the same thread for hand stitching as for machine stitching, unless the stitching is to be decorative as well as functional, when you can use embroidery thread or buttonhole twist in a crewel needle. Cut (rather than break) the length of thread required – 18in is a good length (or 25in for basting) – longer threads encourage tangles. Moisten the end and thread it through the eye. There are various types of needle threaders available to make threading easier.

Thimbles

Steel thimbles are best, and they are available in several sizes. Choose one which fits the middle finger of your sewing hand and push with the side of that finger as you ease the needle through with your thumb and forefinger. With practice this becomes a complete and easy movement on every stitch. A tailor's thimble has no top on it, which encourages the right movement and is cooler on the finger.

Stitching

Any necessary folding, pinning, basting finishing of edges and pressing must be done before starting to stitch. Begin and end the stitching with a hidden knot or a backstitch. As with machine stitching, it is important to have an even tension and to space the stitches evenly. Hold the fabric flat with your fingers underneath and only the thumb on top, moving your hand along as you sew. Instructions for stitching are given for a right-handed person. If you are left-handed, sew in the opposite direction.

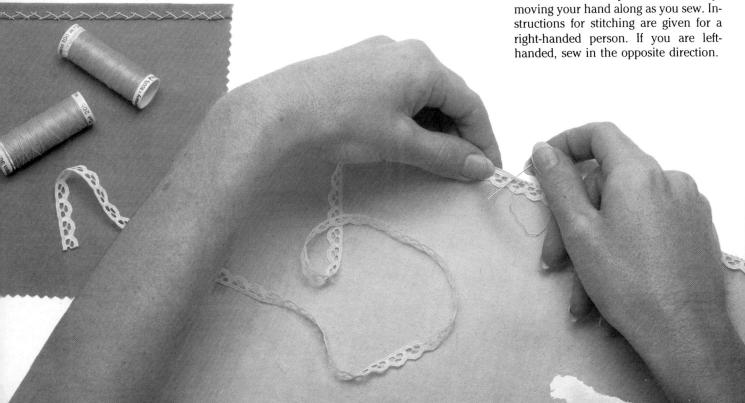

Running stitch

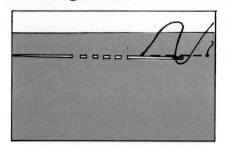

These are small, even stitches used for easing, gathering and for seams on soft fabrics where there is no strain. Working from right to left, take several stitches onto the needle before pulling it through. Take the next series of stitches, keeping them even. Make stitches ⅟₁₆-⅛in long for seams and ⅛-¼in long for gathering.

Backstitch

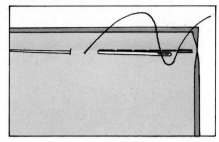

This is a strong, securing stitch used for seams. Working from right to left, insert the needle a stitch length back from where the thread emerges and bring it out a stitch length ahead of that point. Put the needle back into the end of the previous stitch, bringing it out as before. Make stitches ⅟₁₆-⅛in long, with the stitches twice the length on the back.

Prick stitch

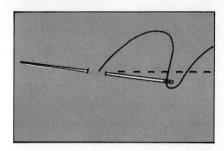

This is made in a similar way to backstitch, but is worked over one or two threads only on the backward stitch. It is used for putting in zippers or securing the ends of bound buttonholes. It can also be used decoratively by stitching a contrasting thread through one layer of fabric with a relaxed tension, so that the small stitches lie on the surface.

Overcasting

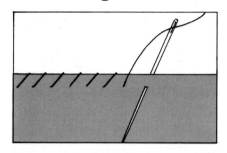

Used for finishing raw edges and preparing hand-worked buttonholes, this stitch can be worked from right or left. Insert the needle into the fabric ⅛in from the raw edge and ¼in from the previous stitch, forming an edge of slanting stitches. On a curving hem, pull the stitches tighter to help ease fullness.

Whipstitch

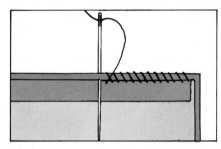

This is used to join lace or ribbon to a folded edge or a selvage. It is worked in a similar way to overcasting, but normally from right to left, catching only one or two threads in each stitch and making stitches closer together, to make a firm, but delicate-looking edge.

Hemming stitch

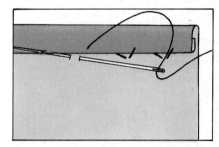

Working from right to left, pick up one or two threads from the garment and insert needle diagonally through the fold of the hem. Pull through. Pick up another two threads from the garment, spacing stitches ¼in apart. Do not pull the stitches too tightly, or they will show on the right side of the garment.

Slipstitch

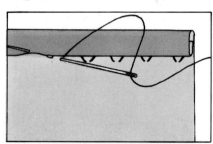

With the fold of the hem toward or away from you (whichever is more comfortable), work this stitch from right to left. Pick up one or two threads from the garment, insert the needle into the fold directly above and slide it along for ⅛-¼in. Pick up one or two threads from the garment, without pulling the stitches too tightly, and repeat.

Catch stitch

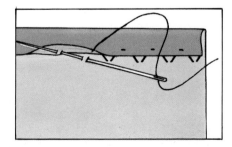

Working from right to left, pick up one or two threads from the garment. With the edge of the hem folded back, insert the needle into the hem and pick up one or two threads. Do not pull the stitches tightly. On stretch fabrics and knits leave a loop of thread ½in long every 4in to give the necessary ease.

Herringbone stitch

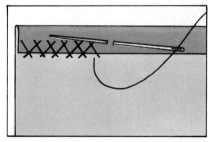

This embroidery stitch is used for securing interfacing and hems on heavier fabrics and is worked from left to right. Take one or two threads from the garment with the needle working from right to left. Then take several threads from the hem or interfacing to the right of the previous stitch, with the needle inserted from right to left.

PATTERNS
Choosing the pattern size

Choosing the right pattern size is the key to making a well-fitting garment. Patterns cannot be exchanged or returned, and by choosing the right size you minimize major alterations and the frustration that often goes with attempting them. Pattern sizes are based on standard body measurements, so your own measurements should be taken carefully and checked from time to time. Sometimes figure proportions change with little or no variation in weight.

Taking your measurements
It is impossible to take your measurements successfully on your own, so enlist the help of a friend. Stand upright, but naturally, in appropriate underwear. The tape measure should be taut around you, but not so tight as to be dishonest. For taking width measurements the tape should be parallel to the floor. A cord tied around your middle settles in your natural waistline if you move around a bit and is a useful guide for taking accurate waist measurements. You should measure:

Height (without shoes): from floor to top of head
Bust: around the fullest part of the bust
Chest: under the arms and above the breasts
Waist: where the cord lies
Hips: around the fullest part of the hips, normally 7-9in below waist
Back waist length: from the prominent bone at the base of the neck to the waist

Measurements for fitting
Extra measurements for fitting are not needed for choosing your pattern size, but you will need many of these measurements to check your pattern for a good fit.

Dress, blouse or skirt
Neck: around the base of the neck
Shoulder: from neck to the point of the shoulder

Back width: across the back between armholes, about 4-6in below the base of the neck
Sleeve length: from top of shoulder, over bent elbow to wrist
Upper arm: around the fullest part of the upper arm, with the elbow bent
Bust point: from the side base of the neck to the bust point
Finished garment length: from the prominent bone at the base of the neck to the required length for dresses and blouses, and from the waist for skirts

Pants
Outside leg: from waist to required length
Inside leg: from crotch to required length
Crotch: sitting on a hard chair, from the side waist to the chair, or from back waist to front waist through the crotch
Thigh: around the widest part of the thigh

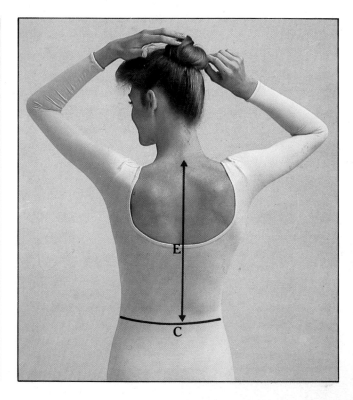

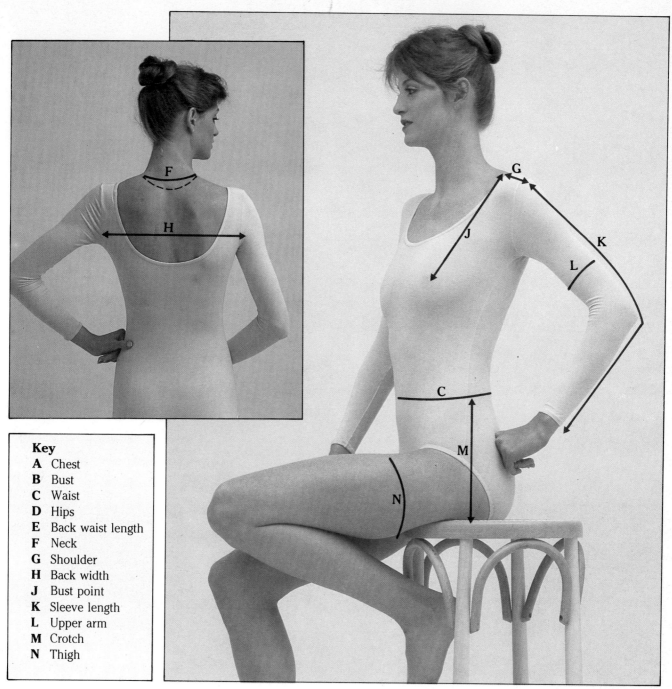

Key
A Chest
B Bust
C Waist
D Hips
E Back waist length
F Neck
G Shoulder
H Back width
J Bust point
K Sleeve length
L Upper arm
M Crotch
N Thigh

Ease

The difference between the body width measurement and the total pattern width at that point is called the ease. Wearing ease is about $2\frac{1}{2}$in on the bust and hips and 1in on the waist, and is the allowance for comfort and movement in the garment. Anything more is the style ease and is a feature of the individual design. Stretch-knit patterns, lingerie and some cut-away styles have little or no wearing ease. Coats, jackets and maternity clothes have more ease, and you should not buy a larger size. (In the case of maternity clothes, the pattern size relates to your size before pregnancy.) Wearing ease varies a little with fashion and among the different pattern companies.

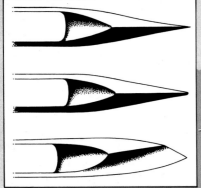

Machine needles and thread
Match the needle point, size and thread with the fabric for the best results.

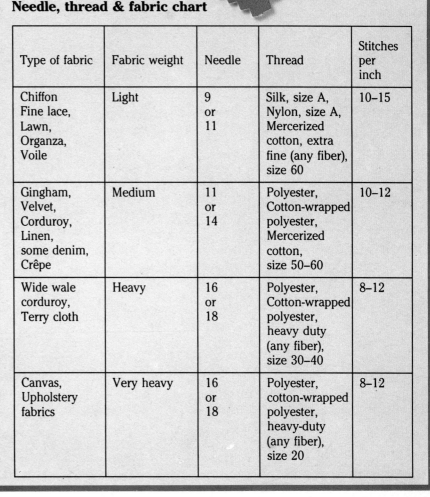

Needle sizes
Different size needles with different points are required for different sewing jobs. Sizes range from 9 to 18. The lowest number is the finest needle. Lightweight fabric requires a fine needle, and a heavyweight fabric a thicker needle to prevent deflection or breakage. Needles specially-treated for synthetic fabrics are available for some machines.

Needle points
It is very important to choose the correct needle point for each fabric. For all types of woven fabric a sharp-point needle (1) is most commonly used. For knitted fabrics use a ball-point needle (2), which separates the fabric rather than piercing it. The wedge-point needle (3) is designed to penetrate leathers and vinyls without splitting the fabric.

Using the wrong needle will affect the stitch formation, and sometimes will prevent stitching completely. Thread will split and fray if a thick needle is used on a fine fabric. The needle should be changed after each garment, or after eight hours of sewing. If a needle is blunt it will cause a thumping sound as it stitches.

Choosing threads
The higher the number stated on the label, the finer the thread. Mercerized cotton or silk thread should be used on cotton or linen, and synthetic thread on man-made fibers. Silk and synthetic threads are capable of stretching and for this reason are ideal for wool fabrics.

If the thread is too heavy for the fabric, it will sit on the surface when stitched, and will wear out quickly. As thread appears lighter when sewn, choose a shade slightly darker than the fabric.

Needle, thread & fabric chart

Type of fabric	Fabric weight	Needle	Thread	Stitches per inch
Chiffon Fine lace, Lawn, Organza, Voile	Light	9 or 11	Silk, size A, Nylon, size A, Mercerized cotton, extra fine (any fiber), size 60	10–15
Gingham, Velvet, Corduroy, Linen, some denim, Crêpe	Medium	11 or 14	Polyester, Cotton-wrapped polyester, Mercerized cotton, size 50–60	10–12
Wide wale corduroy, Terry cloth	Heavy	16 or 18	Polyester, Cotton-wrapped polyester, heavy duty (any fiber), size 30–40	8–12
Canvas, Upholstery fabrics	Very heavy	16 or 18	Polyester, cotton-wrapped polyester, heavy-duty (any fiber), size 20	8–12

Patterns for men

Men's patterns are based on standard body measurements for men of average build and a height of 5ft 10in without shoes. To select the right pattern size you will need to take the appropriate body measurements and compare them with those on the pattern. It is unlikely that the body measurements will coincide exactly with those on the pattern, so choose the size that comes closest to them. If the man is taller than 5ft 10in the pattern will probably need to be lengthened in the main body pieces, sleeves and pant legs (see page 16-17).

Taking measurements
The measurements you need to take will depend on the garment you are making. You need the chest measurement for coats and jackets, neck and sleeve measurements for shirts and the waist measurement for pants.

Measure the man in underwear or a lightweight shirt or T-shirt and pants. Hold the tape measure taut, but not tight, around the body.

Measurements to help choose the pattern size
Height: from floor to top of head without shoes
Neck (A): around the neck at Adam's apple, plus ½in for the neckband size
Chest (B): around fullest part of chest
Waist (C): around the natural waist (where the waistband of his pants normally lies)
Hips (D): around fullest part of seat
Sleeve length (E): from base of neck at center back, along the shoulder to wrist, over a bent elbow

Measurements for fitting
Back neck to waist (F): from the prominent bone at the base of the neck to the waist along spine
Shirt length (G): from base of neck to the finished length
Shoulder (H): from base of neck at one side to the shoulder point
Back width (J): from middle of one underarm, across back, to middle of other underarm
Upper arm (K): around the widest part of the arm with arm bent
Wrist (L): around arm 3in above wrist for cuffs, plus ½in for ease

Measurement for pants
Pants length: outside of leg from the waist to the hem
Inside leg: inside leg from the crotch to the hem

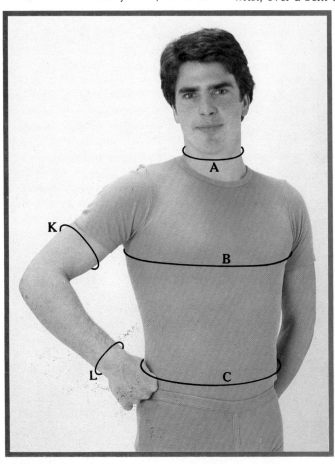

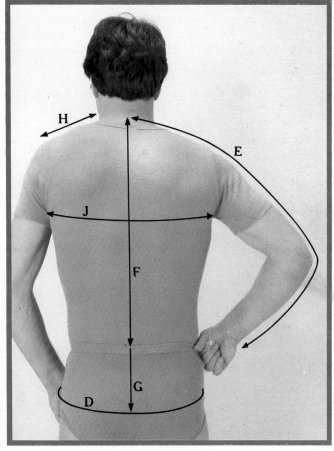

Patterns for children

Children's patterns are sized by age and are based on the standard body measurements. As children's individual body measurements vary so much it is almost impossible to buy a pattern by age and find it fits exactly. Pattern sizings are presented in the following groupings:

Toddlers' $\frac{1}{2}$ – 4
Children's 2 – 6X
Girls' 7 – 14
Boys' 7 – 12

Sizes overlap between groups to allow for changing body proportions. For example, Toddlers' patterns have the same chest and waist measurement as Children's patterns, but are designed for the non-walking child and are shorter in the bodice and slightly narrower on the shoulders. Toddlers' and Children's sizing is suitable for both girls and boys up to size 6, when differences in body proportions demand separate sizings.

Girls' sizes 7 – 14 are designed for the girl who has not yet begun to mature.

Boys' sizes 7 – 12 are for growing boys who have not yet reached full adult stature.

Because of the size differences between the groups, select your pattern by chest and waist measurements, not age, height or weight. It is easy to lengthen or shorten bodices, skirts and sleeves by using the lengthening and shortening lines on the pattern pieces.

WORKBOX

Measurement charts

Toddlers

Size	$\frac{1}{2}$	1	2	3	4
Breast or chest	19	20	21	22	23in
Waist	19	$19\frac{1}{2}$	20	$20\frac{1}{2}$	21in
Finished dress length	14	15	16	17	18in
Approximate height	28	31	34	37	40in

Children

Size	2	3	4	5	6	6X
Breast or chest	21	22	23	24	25	$25\frac{1}{2}$
Waist	20	$20\frac{1}{2}$	21	$21\frac{1}{2}$	22	$22\frac{1}{2}$in
Hip	—	—	24	25	26	$26\frac{1}{2}$in
Back waist length	$8\frac{1}{2}$	9	$9\frac{1}{2}$	10	$10\frac{1}{2}$	11in
Finished dress length	18	19	20	22	24	25in
Approximate height	35	38	41	44	47	48in

Girls

Size	7	8	10	12	14
Breast	26	27	$28\frac{1}{2}$	30	32in
Waist	23	$23\frac{1}{2}$	$24\frac{1}{2}$	$25\frac{1}{2}$	$26\frac{1}{2}$in
Hip	27	28	30	32	34in
Back waist length	$11\frac{1}{2}$	12	13	$13\frac{1}{2}$	14in
Approximate height	50	52	56	$58\frac{1}{2}$	61in

Boys

Size	7	8	10	12
Chest	26	27	28	30in
Waist	23	24	25	26in
Hip	27	28	$29\frac{1}{2}$	31in
Neckband	12	$12\frac{1}{4}$	$12\frac{1}{2}$	13in
Height	48	50	54	58in
Shirt sleeve	$22\frac{1}{2}$	23	25	27in

Ease

There is one important point to remember when determining the child's pattern size. The measurements given for each size are standard body measurements, not measurements of the pattern pieces. To ensure that a garment fits comfortably and smoothly, there has to be a certain amount of ease. This amount will vary at different points in the pattern, as different parts of the body require more or less ease.

Generally the ease allowance in children's patterns is 2in around the chest, 1in at the waist, 2in on the hips, ½in around the base of the neck and 1in around the crotch.

For toddlers, extra ease allowance is allowed for diapers. The amount of ease will vary with the style of the garment and the pattern company. Some pattern companies may allow more ease than others, but this should not affect your choice of pattern.

Measuring children

A good fit begins with the selection of the correct pattern size. To do this, measure the child accurately in underwear and without shoes. Do not pull the tape measure tight. As a child's chest and waist measurements do not differ significantly, it is often difficult to determine where the waistline is, so tie a piece of string around the waistline and let it settle naturally. Alter the pattern where measurements differ.

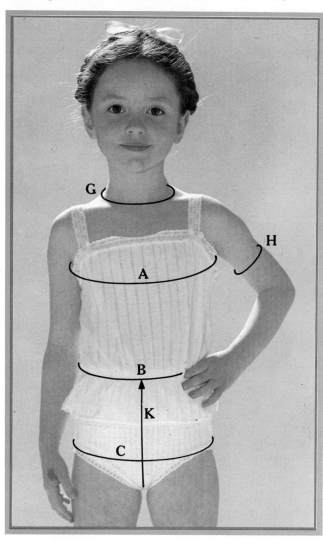

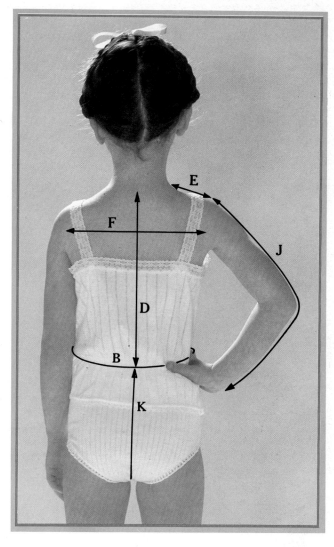

Measurements to help choose the pattern size

Chest (A): around the widest part of the chest

Waist (B): around the natural waist

Hips (C): around the fullest part of the buttocks

Back neck to waist (D): from nape of neck to waist, down center of back

Shoulder width (E): from side of neck to point of shoulder

Back width (F): across back between armholes, about 3in below the base of the neck

Neck (G): around the base of the neck

Upper arm (H): around the fullest part of the upper arm

Arm length (J): from point of shoulder over bent elbow to wrist

Dress length: from nape of neck to finished length

Skirt length: from waist to finished length

Pants

Crotch (K): from back waist under crotch to front waist

Body rise: with child sitting on a hard chair, measure from side waist to chair

Outside leg: from waist to ankle, with shoes on

Inside leg: from crotch to ankle, with shoes on

Thigh: around widest part of thigh

As the proportions of a child's figure change quickly with growth, check the measurements from time to time, especially the length, and alter them accordingly. Make measuring fun by using a child's height chart and marking the increases at regular intervals.

Altering a pattern

Very few people conform to standard sizes. Slight variations can be made at the fitting stage, but a recurring problem may be dealt with more successfully by altering the pattern. Choose a pattern as near to your measurements as possible.

Simple styles can be lengthened or shortened at the hemline, but this can alter the proportions and spoil the design lines. Most patterns have lengthening and shortening lines printed to show where this can be done without changing the style. If not, select places where the alteration will not run through darts, pockets or armholes and draw a line at right angles to the straight grain arrow. Alter bodice length between armhole and waist; sleeves between underarm and elbow, and/or elbow and wrist; skirts at hipline, and/or mid-way between hip and hem; pants between waist and crotch, and/or between crotch and hem.

Darts

After altering darts, fold tissue along dart lines so dart lies in direction it will be pressed. Cut along cutting line at base of dart to shape correctly.

Openings

When lengthening (or shortening) changes the length of an opening, use a longer (or shorter) zipper so that it finishes at the original point. On button openings re-space the placings evenly.

Redrawing

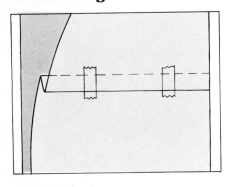

Alterations often result in a jagged step in the pattern line. This must be smoothed out by redrawing a smooth line from above to below the alteration to taper gradually back into the original lines.

Lengthening

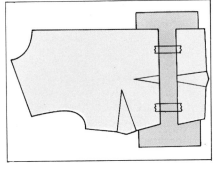

Cut pattern on lengthening line. With cut edges parallel, spread pieces the required distance apart. Insert paper and tape in place. Redraw cutting lines, and dart by joining point to base points.

Shortening

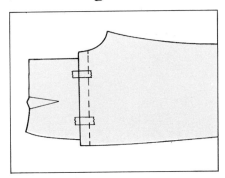

Fold pattern into a parallel pleat along shortening line. The depth of the folded pleat will equal half the amount taken out. Tape in place; redraw cutting lines and dart if necessary.

Altering size

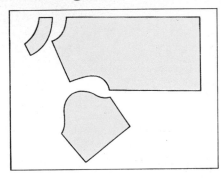

Simple designs which are not closely fitted can be made up to 2in larger by adding an eighth of the increase amount to center front, side front, center back and side back edges. Add the same amount to each side edge of sleeves, and relevant edges of facings. To decrease, subtract in same places.

For large top arm

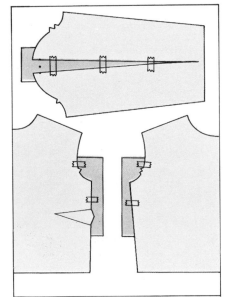

Cut pattern from shoulder point to within ½in of wrist. Insert paper behind slash and spread pattern to increase top arm by required amount. Fix with tape. Mark new shoulder point at center of slash. Lower and increase front and back armholes to increase each by half amount of top sleeve increase. Lower front and back notches to match sleeve notches, measuring from underarm seams to notches.

Before altering pattern pieces, iron out wrinkles with a warm iron. Always mark alterations with felt tip pen or soft pencil to avoid tearing tissue.

Altering waist

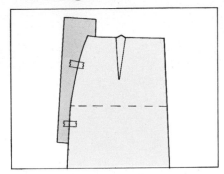

Add a quarter of amount to side edges of front and back. Redraw cutting lines tapering back to original line at hipline. To decrease, reduce in same way. On large increases and decreases move darts half the increase nearer to sides or center respectively. Increase waistband or bodice to correspond.

For sloping shoulders

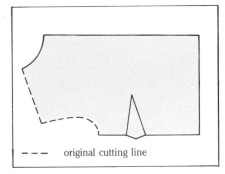

--- original cutting line

On front and back redraw shoulder line from neck to slope down required amount at armhole. Move armhole down and redraw it from new shoulder point to side seam retaining armhole shape and size.

For large bust

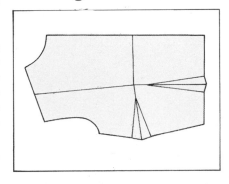

1 Draw lines through center of underarm dart and waist dart to meet at bust point. From bust point draw a line to mid-shoulder and a horizontal line to center front.

Altering hips

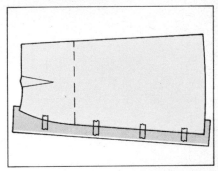

Add a quarter of amount of increase to side edge of front and back at hipline. Redraw cutting line by tapering back to original line at waist and extending line from hip down to hem, keeping the same amount of increase. To decrease, reduce in same way.

For narrow shoulders

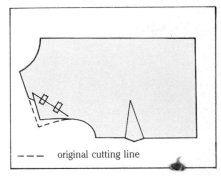

--- original cutting line

Cut front and back from mid-way along shoulder to within ½in of mid-way down armhole. Swivel cut edge to overlap at shoulder, reducing shoulder length by required amount. Fix in place with tape. Redraw shoulder line from neck to shoulder point.

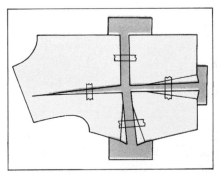

2 Cut along lines and to within ½in of mid-shoulder. Insert paper under pieces to increase half the total required amount. Secure and redraw darts from base to original center length.

17

Enlarging a grid pattern

Enlarging a pattern from a grid is not as difficult as it may first appear. By following a few simple guidelines you will be able to reproduce a pattern easily and accurately. Patterns are generally reproduced to a scale of 1 square = 1in, to correspond to graph paper ruled in inches, or sometimes 1 square = 2in. In this case, it is advisable to darken every other line on 1-inch graph paper to make a clear 2-inch grid. If the scale is not given in whole inches, you can make your own grid on brown paper. Make sure you have a long ruler or a yardstick and a right-angled triangle. You will also need felt-tipped pens, pattern paper and masking tape.

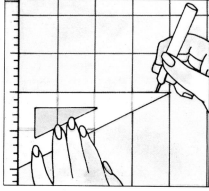

1 *To make your own grid, draw the same number of squares as there are on the original grid, but to the enlarged size. Make the vertical lines first, and then the horizontal lines, with the help of a triangle.*

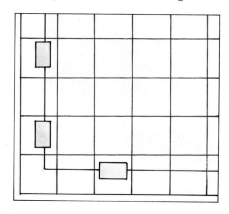

2 *The pattern can now be drawn directly on the enlarged grid, or you can attach a large piece of tissue or pattern paper to it with masking tape so that the basic grid can be used again. This is especially useful if there are several pattern pieces.*

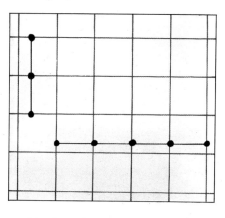

3 *Number horizontal and vertical lines on both grids, to correspond. Reproduce the straight lines of the pattern first, marking the points where they cross the lines of the grid as accurately as possible on the enlarged grid. Join these points with a ruler.*

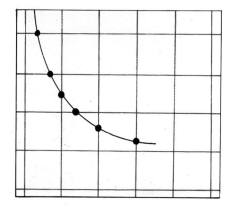

4 *Reproduce curves by marking all the points where the curve intersects the lines of the grid, as accurately as possible. Join the points using a French curve or a flexible curve (available from art shops) for a smooth line.*

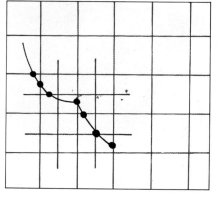

5 *When dealing with intricate shapes, it may help to subdivide the squares by drawing lines through the center of each square on the original and the enlarged grid. In this way you will be able to mark more points, and the line will be more accurate.*

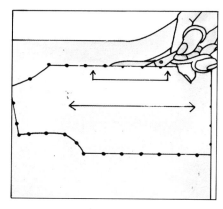

6 *Check the enlarged pattern carefully against the original, counting the squares on each as a double check before removing the paper from the grid. Mark any additional details such as straight grain lines, circles and general instructions. Continue until all the pattern pieces have been scaled up, and then cut them out.*

CUTTING AND FITTING
Cutting out

Although you will be eager to start stitching, always take the time to prepare your fabric and lay out pattern pieces carefully before cutting out. Mistakes can be expensive!

Selecting your fabric
Always choose a good quality fabric which is suitable for the garment you are making. Advice on choice of fabric is given on most commercial patterns. If you are a beginner, choose a light to medium-weight fabric which does not fray easily and is not slippery. Always check washing instructions when buying the fabric, as some fabrics need to be dry-cleaned, and check for crease-resistance by crushing the fabric in your hand.

Fabric grain
Fabrics are woven with strong warp threads lengthwise, and weft threads across the width. The selvage is formed where the weft threads turn back. The "lengthwise grain" or "straight grain" of the fabric is the direction of the warp threads and is parallel to the selvage. The strength of the fabric is in this direction. The "crosswise grain" is the direction of the weft threads, and the fabric has a little give here. "Bias" is any direc-

tion not on the grain, with "true bias" at 45° to both lengthwise and crosswise grains. The fabric has the greatest stretch on the true bias. The direction of grain is the same for knitted fabrics. Weft knit fabric is constructed with the thread looped crosswise and the stretch across the fabric. In warp knit fabric the loops are formed lengthwise.

Straightening cut edges

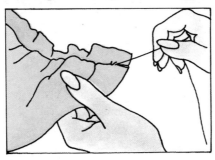

To straighten the cut edges on plain weave wools and linens, clip into the selvage and tweeze out a crosswise thread. Withdraw it little by little, cutting along the space left until you reach the other selvage.

Where it is difficult to withdraw threads, place a right-angled triangle on one selvage. Butt a yardstick against this edge, draw along it with tailor's chalk and cut.

 Avoid fabrics with a regular pattern printed off-grain, as you will need to follow the pattern, not the grain, when cutting, and the finished garment will not hang correctly.

Prepare the paper pattern by cutting out all the necessary pieces, leaving margins outside the cutting line. Smooth pieces with a cool iron.

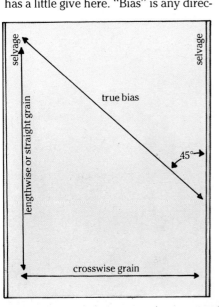

Off-grain fabric

The hang of the finished garment depends on each pattern piece being placed correctly in relation to the grain of the fabric. If the warp and weft threads are not at right angles to each other, the fabric is off-grain and will need to be straightened. Pull at opposite corners, until the fabric is rectangular. Press to remove creases.

Preparing your fabric

Press the fabric to remove creases and mark any flaws with crossed pins so you can avoid them. Let knit fabrics lie flat for an hour to settle before pinning and cutting. If you are in doubt as to the right side of the fabric and it is impossible to see a difference, choose one side and mark every piece you cut with crossed pins.

 Work on a large, flat surface such as the floor or a table. Avoid letting fabric hang over the edge of a table – especially with stretch fabrics – by rolling up one end and then rolling from the other as pattern pieces are pinned in position.

Laying out pattern pieces

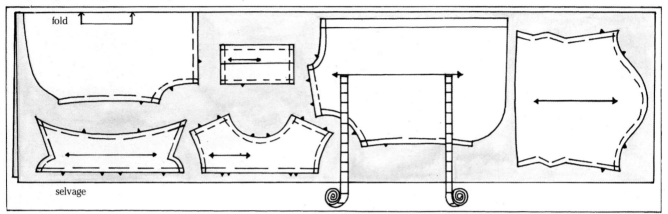

Choose the layout for the pattern view, size and fabric width. Pattern pieces are placed right side up on the fabric unless shown otherwise. Fold the fabric right sides together, lengthwise or crosswise as shown. If the layout shows both lengthwise and crosswise folds, make the crosswise fold first and pin pieces in position, and then make the lengthwise fold, without cutting the fabric. If a pattern piece extends beyond the fold, cut out the other pieces and then open out

the fabric. Always use single layer fabric right side up.

Pin the main pieces first, with lines marked "place on fold" exactly on the fold. Check that the whole length of any straight grain line is parallel to the selvages with a tape measure, and pin along the line. Pin corners of the pattern next, then the edge, keeping pins within seam allowances. Place pins 3–4in apart, at right angles to the cutting line on heavier fabrics and parallel

to the cutting line on lightweight fabrics. Pattern margins may overlap, to save fabric, but never cutting lines. If a pattern piece is used more than once, pin it in place, mark around it with tailor's chalk, and then pin it in other position. Most pattern pieces are the right-hand side of the relevant shape. If the whole shape is needed, trace the pattern on folded tracing paper with the "place on fold" line on the fold. Cut and open out, transferring markings.

Layouts for fabric with nap

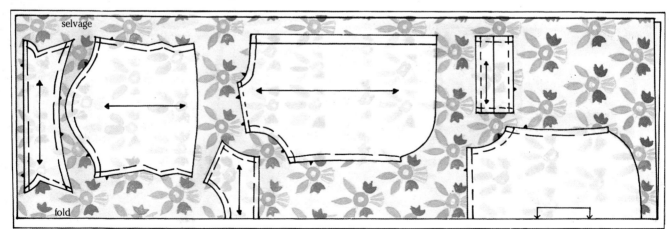

Layouts for fabric with nap should be followed when you are using napped fabrics such as velvet and corduroy, fabrics such as satin, which look different when seen from different directions because of their weave, or fabrics

with a one-way design. The pattern pieces are arranged so that they all lie in the same direction, which ensures that the pile or design runs in one direction on the finished garment.

Crosswise folds cannot be used

because the nap or design would run in opposite directions on matching pieces. Instead, cut the fabric where the fold would be, and turn and pin one piece to the other right sides together, so the design runs the same way on both.

20

Matching striped and plaid fabric

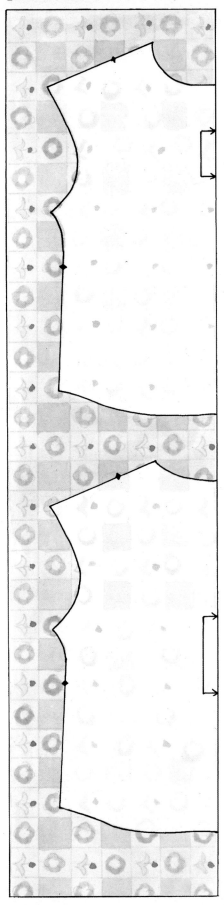

Stripes, plaids and checks larger than $\frac{1}{2}$in should match at the seams. Use a layout for fabric with nap if the design looks different one way up and the other. Some weaves look striped – especially twill weave, which looks like diagonal stripes – and should be treated as striped. Avoid patterns with too many seams or darts, as this will make matching more difficult and confuse the overall effect. Some patterns are designated unsuitable for stripes, diagonal stripes or plaids, if a visual balance of stripes is difficult to achieve.

Stripes should meet at the side seams, center front and back seams, shoulders, top of sleeves and, if possible, over the armhole seams. Position the pattern pieces carefully on the fabric to ensure that they match. Align matching notches on the same stripes or part of check, and make sure that pieces match at the seamline rather than at the cutting line. If necessary, adapt the layout slightly. Try not to place dominant stripes on bust, waist, hip or hemlines. Make all fitting alterations before cutting out, and baste and stitch all seams carefully to ensure a perfect match.

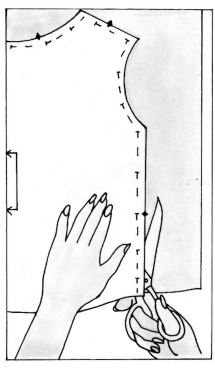

Cutting out

Check you have all the pieces laid out correctly on the fabric before cutting out. Keep one hand on the fabric and use long, firm strokes along the cutting line, cutting notches outward. Keep scraps of fabric for testing stitch tensions.

The following samples of napped and patterned fabric are examples of fabrics which need to be handled with care when cutting out.

Cotton corduroy

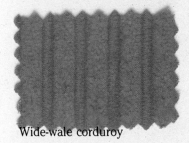

Wide-wale corduroy

Polyester-cotton slub

Yarn-dyed cotton

Printed striped cotton

21

Marking the fabric

The notches, dots and lines on the pattern are there to enable you to match pattern pieces correctly and sew accurately. Once you have cut out the pattern, transfer these marks to the fabric with the pattern pieces still pinned in place. Work on a hard, flat surface to prevent crooked lines and misplaced dots. Experiment on scraps of fabric with the different methods and gadgets available to find the most effective method.

1 Tailor's chalk
2 Tracing wheel
3 Basting thread
4 Chalk pad with circular guide
5 Yardstick
6 Chalk pencils and marking pencil
7 Ruler
8 Right-angled triangle

Chalk

Chalk is available in pencil form, or as a flat cake, which can be sharpened against an open scissor blade. A useful device for marking double layers of fabric is a chalk pad with circular guide. Test on a scrap of fabric to see if it can be removed by brushing or wiping with a damp sponge before using on the right side of the fabric. Always choose a color close to that of the fabric.

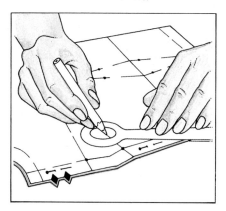

To mark one layer of fabric, put a pin through pattern and fabric and mark with a cross. To mark a double layer, slide the chalk pad under the fabric and the circular guide over the point to be marked on the pattern. Mark the top with a chalk pencil and the bottom layer will be marked automatically. Mark lines by moving the guide along and making a series of dashes.

Using dressmaker's carbon paper and a tracing wheel

This method is most successful on smooth fabrics. Use white carbon paper on light colored fabrics and a harmonizing color with darker ones. Always use on the wrong side of the fabric and test to make sure that it does not show through to the right side.

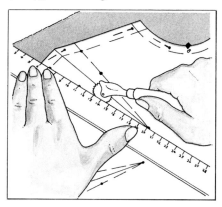

To mark single-layer fabric, place the carbon paper colored side down on the wrong side of the fabric, with the pattern pinned in place on top. Hold firmly in place and trace along straight lines using a tracing wheel and ruler. Mark dots with a cross.

To mark two layers of fabric, place one piece of carbon paper, colored side down, on the top layer of fabric under the pattern, and a second piece, colored side up, under the bottom layer. Press firmly on the tracing wheel when tracing the markings, but be careful not to damage the fabric.

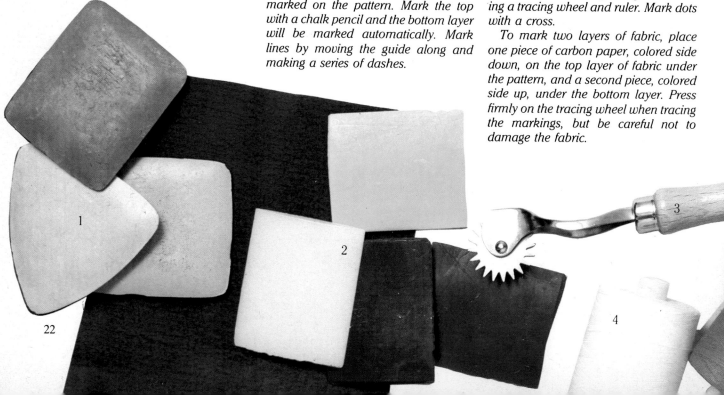

Tailor's tacks

Tailor's tacks are the best method to use when marking the right side of the fabric, and can be used on napped or delicate fabrics, which might be damaged by other methods. Use them to mark the position of pockets, pleats, darts and tucks.

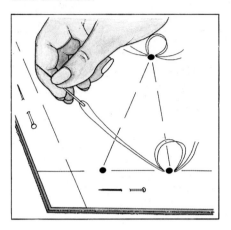

1 *Sew through pattern and both layers of fabric, using a length of doubled, unknotted thread. Leaving a 1in end, backstitch into same point to make a loop and cut, leaving an end.*

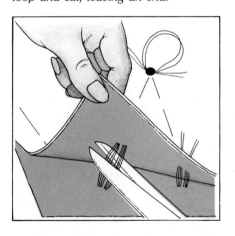

2 *When all dots have been marked, gently separate the layers of fabric as far as the loops permit and cut threads at the center, taking care not to cut the fabric. Cut through top loop and remove pattern piece.*

Lines of tailor's tacks

These are a simplified version of tailor's tacks and can be used to mark seamlines, fold lines, darts and pleats on single or double fabric. If your pattern piece has more than one set of markings, use different colored threads to avoid confusion.

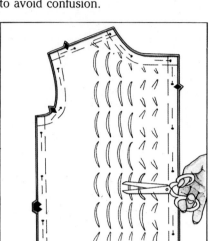

With a long double thread, take a stitch into the fabric on the pattern line, leaving an end of 1in. Continue making long, loose stitches on the surface of the pattern and short stitches through the pattern and fabric as necessary. Mark all the pattern lines in this way and then cut the thread at the center of each long surface stitch and remove pattern gently. When working through two layers of fabric, separate the layers without pulling out the stitches and clip the threads between layers as before, to leave short ends in each layer.

 Basting thread is ideal for tailor's tacks. This is not as smooth as other threads and is less likely to slip out of the fabric.

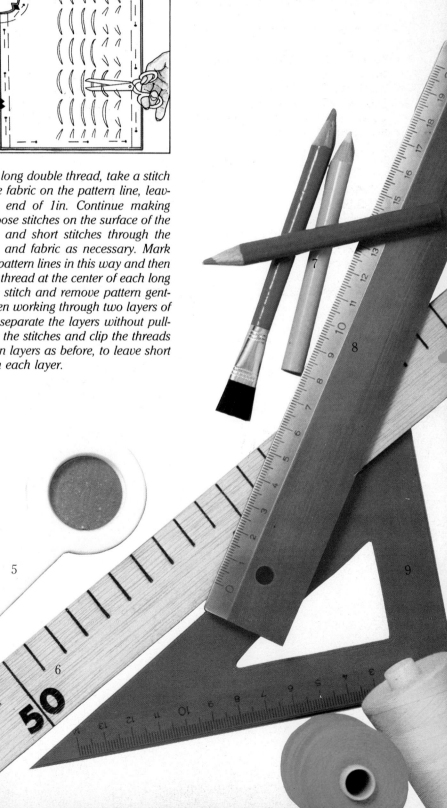

Threads

A wide choice of threads is available, in fiber, color and thickness. For normal sewing, choose a color which matches, or is a shade darker than the dominant color of the fabric.

Threads normally come on spools of 125 or 325yd, but silk and the thicker threads have less on each spool. Some basic colors, such as black and white are available on larger spools. The color ranges and also the thickness of cotton-coated polyester vary between brands. Look before you buy. Consider the weight of the fabric when choosing the thickness of the thread, and use the appropriate needle size.

General sewing threads

1 Mercerized cotton is a smooth, shiny, strengthened cotton, for sewing natural fibers. Cotton thread has no give in it and so is unsuitable for sewing knits or stretch fabrics. It is widely available in sizes 50 (fine) and 40 (thicker). A very few colors are available in size 60. Soft unmercerized cotton is used for basting.

2 Cotton-coated polyester combines the strength of a polyester thread with the non-stretch properties of cotton. It is, therefore, suitable for non-stretch fabrics, both natural and man-made. Very fine cotton-polyester, called lingerie thread, is suitable for delicate fabrics. There is also a strong thick thread used for heavy-duty sewing.

3 Polyester is a fine thread used on fabrics made of synthetic fibers and available in a wide color range. It is a stretchy thread, particularly suitable for knits, other stretch fabrics, and woven man-made fabrics. When used for hand sewing has a tendency to knot.

Special purpose threads

4 Buttonhole twist is available in both polyester for synthetic fabric and silk for natural fabric. It is thicker and stronger than normal thread and is used for thread loops, hand-worked buttonholes on medium to heavyweight fabrics and decorative topstitching.

5 Fine silk is ideal for basting because it can be pressed without marking. It is a strong, elastic thread, used on natural fibers.

6 Machine embroidery threads are cotton threads, available in solid and variegated colors. The latter is one continuous thread, dyed in lengths of contrasting or harmonizing colors.

7 Metallic silver, gold, brass and mixed metallic colors are available, though they come and go with fashion. These threads are used for decorative stitching, by hand or machine.

Hand embroidery threads (not shown) include: six-strand embroidery floss, *coton à broder* (a shiny, smooth-finish thread), pearl cotton (a twisted, lustrous thread) and matte embroidery cotton.

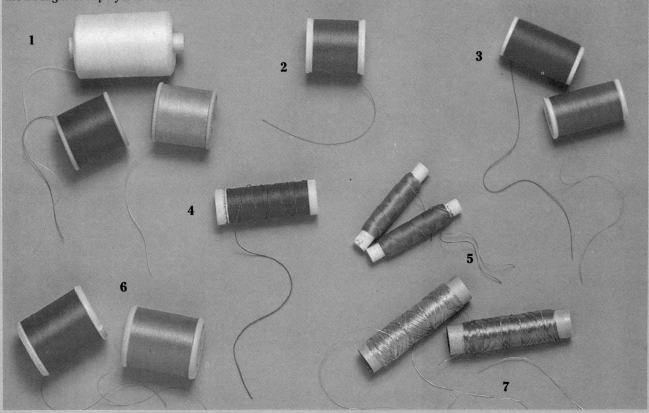

Pinning and basting

Pinning and basting are the first stages of making a garment. Basting holds the fabric in place temporarily until permanent stitching is completed. It will prevent fabric layers from slipping and is essential if you are stitching through several layers (on collars or waistbands for example), or matching a fabric design. It also allows you to check the fit of the garment.

Use basting thread for hand basting and remove it before pressing to avoid leaving an imprint on the fabric. Use silk thread on delicate fabrics and when basting pleats for pressing. Baste close to the seamline and then machine stitch, following the basting line.

Different basting stitches

Uneven basting This is used to mark fabric, or to hold two layers together, especially on straight seams, where there will be little or no strain on the stitches.

Even basting This should be used where more secure stitching is needed, especially on curves, for fitting, and for matching a fabric design.

Matching a design

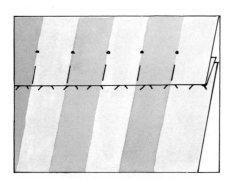

Turn under the seam allowance on one edge and press. Place seamlines together and pin, matching the pattern. On the right side, slip the needle through the fold, then through the fabric on the other seamline, making ¼in stitches to hold the design firmly in line.

Staystitching This is a reinforcing stitch used to prevent stretching on curves such as necklines and armholes and on loosely woven or stretch fabrics. It also strengthens clipped seams.

Uneven basting

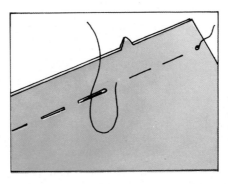

Knot the basting thread and make uneven stitches about 1in apart. To save time, pick up several stitches at once before pulling the needle through the fabric.

Even basting

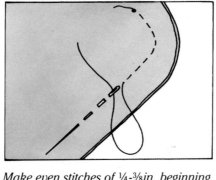

Make even stitches of ¼-⅜in, beginning and ending with a backstitch.

Easestitching This is a reasonably long stitch, often used on shoulders, sleeve caps and waistlines as a means of pulling up extra fabric without creating gathers or tucks.

Easestitching

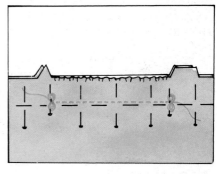

Make one row of stitching on single layer fabric, just inside the seamline. Pin at regular intervals, matching notches and circles. Pull up the thread and distribute the extra fabric evenly. Finish pinning and baste, gently easing the fullness in without forming gathers.

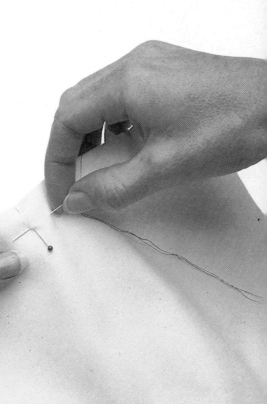

Straight seams

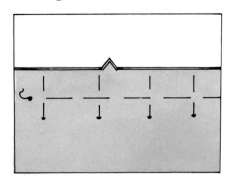

Place fabric pieces right sides together, matching notches, and pin at right angles to the seamline. This makes it easier to distribute any extra fabric, and with practice you can stitch without basting or removing pins (if the machine permits). Baste close to the seamline.

Curved seams

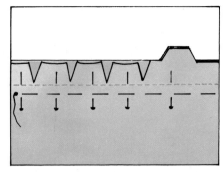

Staystitch within the seam allowance, ⅛in from the seamline, using a normal machine stitch. Check the curve against the pattern for stretching and pull up the thread slightly to ease into shape. Clip the fabric to make it lie flat, and pin, matching notches. Baste.

Angled seams

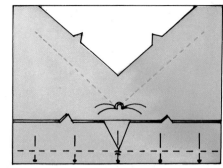

Staystitch just inside the seamline with a small machine stitch. Clip into the angle and pin as shown, matching notches and circles. Baste along seamline, making an extra backstitch at the base of the angle to hold it firmly.

WORKBOX

Functional stitches

Functional stitches are primarily practical stitches used for construction rather than decoration, though some can be used decoratively as well. Experiment with different stitch sizes to suit your fabric.

1 Straight stitch for most seams

2 Zigzag stitch for finishing raw edges

3 Satin stitch for appliqué and buttonholes

4 Three-step zigzag (tricot) for finishing edges of knits and difficult fabrics, and applying elastic

5 Stretch stitch for very strong seams, and bold topstitching

6 Blind hemming for machine-stitched hems

7 Stretch overcasting for stitching and finishing narrow seams in one operation

8 Fly stitch for butt-joining two non-fray edges, such as leather

BASIC GARMENT CONSTRUCTION
Sewing a plain seam

Plain, open seams are the basis of most dressmaking, so learn to sew, press and finish them with confidence. Finished seams prevent fraying and help the hang of the garment. Only a few non-fraying fabrics, such as knits, and lined garments do not need finished seams.

Preparing to stitch
Choose a needle and thread appropriate to the fabric and try out different stitch lengths on a double layer of fabric. Always press the stitching. Too short a stitch pulls the fabric, while too long a stitch leads to gaping and wrinkles. The

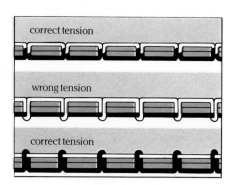

correct tension

wrong tension

correct tension

knot of the machine stitch should be in the middle of the doubled layer of fabric, not on the top or bottom. If you have the right needle, thread and stitch

Stitching the seam
When the fabric is pinned and basted, put the needle into the fabric three or four stitch lengths away from the raw edge and lower the presser foot. Hold the free ends of the threads as you begin to sew so that they do not disappear around the bobbin. Stitch backward first, then forward steadily along the

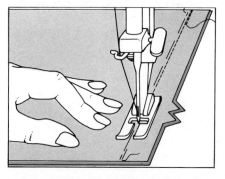

basting but not directly over it, as this makes it difficult to remove. The basting is your guide to sewing a straight line, but you should keep the raw edges of the fabric on the appropriate line on the needle plate (marked at $\frac{1}{8}$in intervals) as a double check. The machine will automatically sew straight, so the fabric only needs guidance and support. Guide the fabric gently with your hand in front of the needle, rather than pulling and pushing. Never impede the nor-

mal feeding process.

If you are sewing through several layers, like a crotch seam, you may have to help the fabric through a little more. With bias seams on stretch fabric it is easy to let the fabric stretch as you stitch, so support the fabric before it reaches the needle. Stitch at a reasonable speed and practice controlling the speed accurately. At the end of the seamline, stitch backward over three stitches. Avoid overshooting the edge of the fabric before backstitching, as this causes puckers. To be secure, the stitches must be on top of one another.

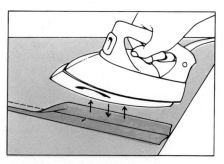

Raise the presser foot and pull the work toward the back of the machine. Cut the threads about 4in from the needle with a pair of small, sharp scissors. Press the seam flat as stitched, and then open and press with a steam iron, or a dry iron and damp cloth.

length, you should rarely need to alter the tension to achieve this. Knit fabrics should be stitched with a ball-point needle and a zigzag stitch. The zigzag width should be just off zero so that it looks like straight stitch, but gives a little more stretch in the stitching to match the flexible fabric.

 Many patterns have arrows on the seamlines to show in which direction they should be sewn. This will minimize fraying when finishing.

Turned finish

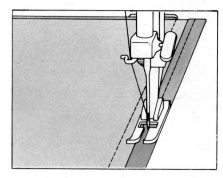

With wrong side facing, turn over ¼in along each raw edge. Press. Stitch with a normal length stitch, and press again. This method is particularly good for finishing fine fabrics.

 Always knot and clip the ends of the threads as you work. Leave plenty of length when stitching a seam, tie a knot as close to the seam as possible and clip. If the machine stitching line does not reach the seam edge, pull the top thread through to the wrong side with the help of a pin, then knot both threads together, and clip as before.

Overcast finish

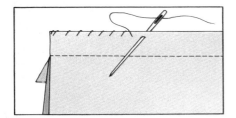

Overcast stitches are ideal for sheer and delicate fabrics and can be used instead of zigzag stitch, if your machine does not have this facility. Hold the raw edge of the fabric away from you and hand sew even diagonal stitches over the raw edge ⅛in into the fabric.

Pinked finish

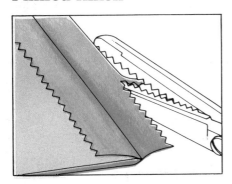

Trimming with pinking shears is a good and quick method of finishing seams on firmly woven fabric. Trim along the raw edge, cutting away only small triangles of fabric.

Zigzag finish

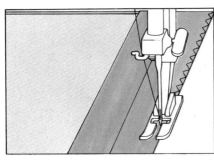

This is a particularly good method for edges that tend to fray. Experiment beforehand to find the correct stitch length and width. Generally a fine fabric needs a narrow stitch and a heavier fabric a wide one. Align the outer edge of the zigzag stitch with the raw edge of the fabric. This is also a good method of finishing seams together – especially on curved seams such as armholes and crotches, where it also strengthens the seam. It is not suitable if the raw edge rolls within the zigzag.

French seams

1 *Place the fabric pieces wrong sides together, with raw edges even. Stitch ⅜in in from edge and trim seam allowance to about ⅛in.*

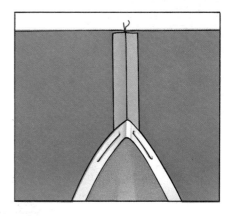

2 *Open out flat, then using just the tip of the iron, press the seam open. Turn fabric wrong side up and press flat along the seamline.*

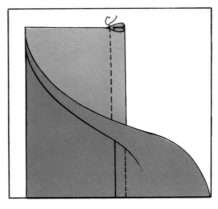

3 *Re-fold with right sides together. With first seam at edge, make a second line of stitching ¼in from fold, making sure you enclose the raw edges.*

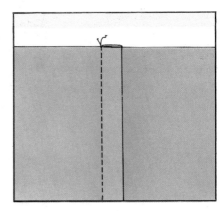

4 *Open the seam out flat, and with the wrong side facing, press the finished seam toward the back of the garment using the tip of the iron only.*

Double-stitched seam

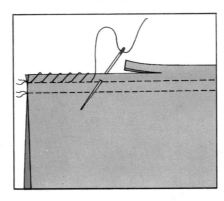

Stitch a plain seam, then make a second row of stitching ¼in away, within seam allowance. Trim close to second row of stitching. Finish by overcasting or whipping edge finely.

Self-bound seam

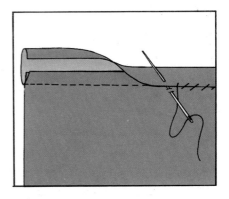

Stitch a plain seam along usual stitching line. Trim one seam allowance to ¼in. Turn opposite edge over twice to enclose the raw edge and hem in place along seamline.

Curved seams

Stitching a good curve really depends on your ability to guide your fabric and control the speed at which you sew, so practice on scraps of fabric until you feel confident. Joining similar curves (on collars or necklines for example) is not difficult if you follow a few simple rules. Match raw edges and pin and baste pieces together carefully. Baste along the seamline using small, even basting stitches and then machine stitch slowly and carefully, using the basting line as a guide and keeping the foot a constant distance from the raw edges of the fabric. Opposite curves require a little more care and will need to be eased together as you sew. Always staystitch both curves to prevent their stretching. The plain curved seam will shape a garment discreetly, whereas the topstitched curved seam can be used as a decorative feature to emphasize the lines of a design.

Always trim the seam allowances to half width and clip or notch to reduce bulk and allow the seam to lie flat to give a smooth curve.

By grading the seam allowances on an enclosed seam you can prevent a ridge from showing on the right side of the garment. Simply trim each seam allowance to a different width to produce a layered effect, making sure that the wider seam allowance falls next to the outside of the garment.

Inward curves

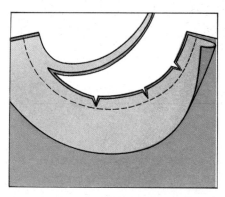

Match the raw edges of similar inward curves, and pin and baste carefully along the seamline before machine stitching. Trim seam allowances to half width and clip by cutting right up to the stitching with the point of small, sharp scissors, taking care not to cut the stitching. Clip at regular intervals, just frequently enough for the fabric to spread to allow the seam to lie in position without pulling and distorting the curve.

Outward curves

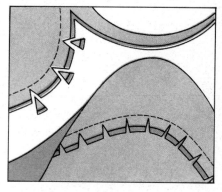

Match the raw edges of similar outward curves and pin, baste and stitch carefully along the seamline. Trim seam allowances to half width and cut small V-shaped notches on outward curves which will be pressed to form an inward curve (on a collar for example). Notching is only necessary when a clipped seam allowance would overlap and cause a lumpy seam. Clip or notch fraying fabrics in different places.

Joining opposite curves

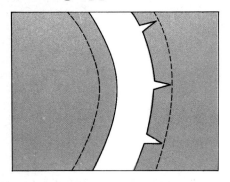 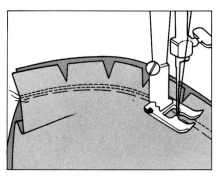 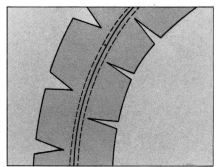

1 *Staystitch both curves by machine stitching within the seam allowance, ⅛in from the seamline. Clip the seam allowance on edge of inward curve at regular intervals to allow the curve to spread to match the outward curve.*

2 *Place the two pieces right sides together, matching seamlines, with the clipped curve on top. Pin at right angles to the raw edge and baste along the seamline using small, even basting stitches. Stitch, using basting as guide.*

3 *Press the seam as stitched and then press open using the tip of the iron only. Cut notches from the unclipped edge so that the seam allowances lie flat to each side of the seam. Press again.*

Topstitched curved seam

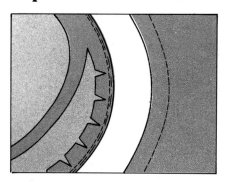

1 *Reinforce both curves with stay-stitching. Fold under the seam allowance on the outward curve and baste along the folded edge. Press carefully to give a good curve. Trim the seam allowance to half width and cut notches to the staystitching.*

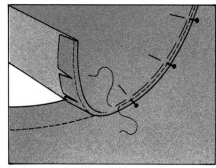

2 *With right sides uppermost, place the outward curve on top of the inward curve, aligning the folded edge with the seamline. Pin at right angles to the seam and baste in place, using small, even basting stitches. With right sides uppermost, topstitch through all thicknesses. Press.*

Pressing

Keep your iron and ironing board nearby as you sew, so that you can press at each stage of assembling the garment to obtain a professional finish. A good pressing technique is as necessary to the finished appearance of the garment as expert sewing. One final press is not enough.

Your equipment should include a clean, medium-weight iron, an ironing board with a smooth, well-fitting cover, and one or more pressing cloths. A piece of batiste or lawn will usually serve the purpose, but you may also need a heavier cotton cloth and a flannel one. Avoid fabric with holes or a prominent grain, which would mark the fabric, and wash to remove any finish that may be present. A dry cloth may prevent water marks when using a steam iron.

Different fabrics need different treatment, so experiment with different pressure, heat and moisture (steam and/or a damp cloth) on scraps of your fabric. In general, man-made fibers need less heat than natural fibers.

Straight seams

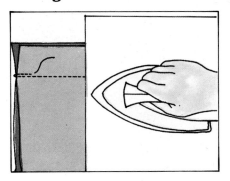

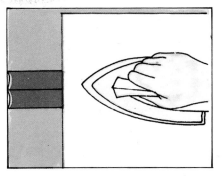

1 *Remove pins and basting before pressing to avoid leaving indentations in the fabric. Pins will also scratch your iron. Press the seam flat, as stitched, using a damp (not wet) or dry press cloth, to embed the stitches.*

2 *Now open out the seam allowances and press open, still using a press cloth, by lifting and lowering the iron onto the garment, rather than running it over the fabric, as you would normally do in ironing.*

Where it is impossible to press from the wrong side of the fabric, press from the right side, using a press cloth to prevent overpressing and shiny marks.

Curved seams

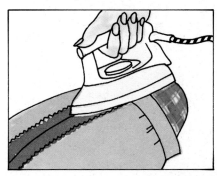

Press curved seams on a rounded surface. A pressing mitt or tailor's ham is a useful aid, but you can press over the end of the board with the tip of your iron.

Napped fabrics

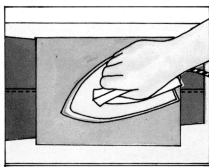

Press napped fabrics from the wrong side on a towel or needleboard so as not to crush the pile. When pressing from the right side, use a spare piece of fabric as a press cloth, and place the two piled surfaces together.

Pressing equipment

Always have your pressing equipment at hand before you start any serious sewing – an item that's well pressed has a much more professional finish. Different pieces of equipment are useful for pressing different areas of a garment.

1 Iron The best type is a combination dry and steam iron, because it can deal with so many different types of fabric – but you can use an ordinary dry iron with a moist press cloth.

2 Ironing board Make sure it's well padded with no lumps and bumps to make marks on the fabric. It should be adjustable to different heights so that you can sit or stand comfortably to use it. You will also need a sleeve board.

3 Sleeve board A useful mini ironing board that clips onto the main one and enables you to get into awkward places such as sleeves and shoulder seams.

4 Tailor's ham You may not have heard of this one. It's a ham-shaped, firmly stuffed pillow, invaluable for pressing curved areas like darts and shoulder seams. Easy to make yourself.

5 Pressing mitt Again for awkward places, but it's a well padded mitt that you slip over your hand, rather like an oven mitt.

6 Seam roll A narrow sausage-shaped pillow for pressing seams, which is easy to make. Because it's narrow and rounded you press only the seam and don't make any lines elsewhere.

7 Point presser A narrow wooden board pointed at one end for points in collars, waistbands, etc.

8 Needleboard A piece of canvas covered with short, fine wire bristles for pressing fabrics with a pile, such as velvet.

9 Tailor's clapper To help you flatten faced edges and seams. It's a piece of wood you literally pound the seams with. Use a damp press cloth and make lots of steam, then slap the seam with the board while it's still damp.

10 Pressing cloths In three different weights (soft muslin, white flannel and a heavy firm white cotton), all about 25×15in.

11 Brown paper Put strips under seams and edges of pleats to prevent ridges from showing through on the right side.

12 Clothes brush Useful to remove threads and fluff from items as you press them, and for lifting the nap on velvet, corduroy, etc.

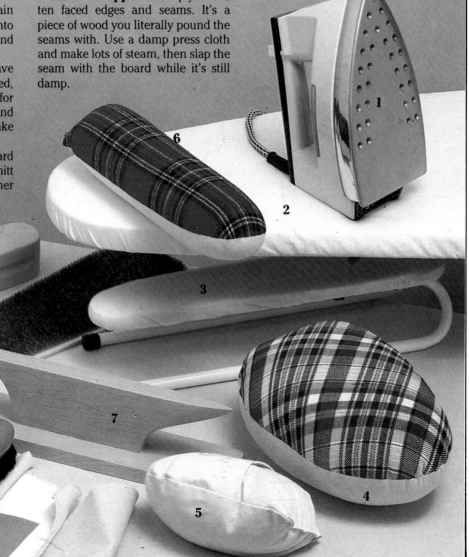

Darts

Darts are tapered tucks which give shape to a garment by controlling fullness for a good and comfortable fit. Darts point to the fullest part of the bust and the curve of the hips, where extra width is needed. Shoulder darts give ease over the back, and sleeve darts ease over the elbow in a fitted sleeve. Always check the position of darts before cutting out the fabric. Make any other necessary adjustments to length or width of the pattern first and then pin darts together along the lines of the pattern and hold against the body. Before you stitch, check that matching darts are in the same relative position and are the same length. Slight differences can be very noticeable on fabrics with stripes or a regular pattern.

To give a good fit, stitch darts in a gentle curve to follow the curves of the body. This means that waist-to-hip darts should curve a little toward the fold while waist-to-bust darts should curve a little away from it. Always taper darts gently to the fold at the point to prevent the bubble that forms if the dart reaches the fold too abruptly. If you finish the dart by reverse stitching, make sure that the reverse stitches are exactly on top of the previous stitching to keep a good point. If you find that the fabric puckers at the point, try leaving long ends and knotting together, taking care not to pull the stitching. Sew in the ends by hand on fine fabrics.

Stitching a straight dart

1 *Transfer the markings from the pattern tissue to the fabric, using the method most suited to your fabric (see pages 22–23). Mark all the dots and make a note whether the stitching lines between them are straight or curved.*

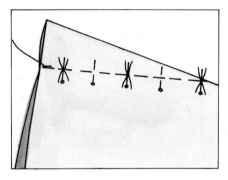

2 *Fold the fabric right sides together along the middle of the dart and put pins through the dots to match them up. Pin at right angles to the stitching line and baste. Remove tailor's tacks before stitching.*

To tie the ends of the threads, place a pin at the point of the dart and tie the threads around it. The knot will slide down the pin and tighten exactly at the point of the dart.

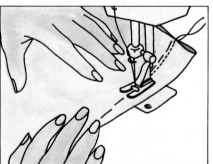

3 *Stitch from the wide end of the dart, tapering gradually to the fold line so that the last two or three stitches fall on the edge of the fold. Finish by reverse stitching, knotting or sewing in the ends. Press as stitched.*

Double-pointed dart

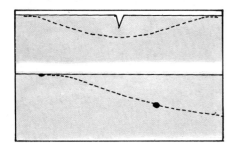

Mark the dart and fold right sides together, matching dots. Pin and baste in the same way as a straight dart. Stitch from each end, beginning and ending with two or three stitches on the fold. Alternatively, stitch from the middle to each point. Clip the widest part of the dart to make it lie flat and press as stitched.

Wide dart

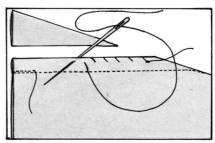

Mark and stitch the dart in the normal way and trim to ½in from the stitching to reduce bulk. Do not cut right to the point as this weakens the fabric. Finish raw edges by overcasting and press open, flattening the point. Wide double-pointed darts must be cut along the fold, edges finished, and pressed open. Again, do not cut right to point.

Curved dart

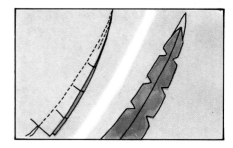

Curved darts are marked with a solid line down the center for slashing. Cut to the end of the marking, not to the point. Reinforce the point by stitching just inside the stitching lines. Match the dots, easing or stretching one side to match the other as indicated. Pin, baste and stitch as before. Press open, clipping to prevent puckering, and flatten the point.

Pressing

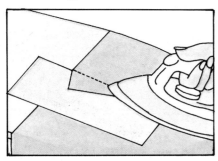

1 Always press darts open or to one side before stitching main seams. Press vertical darts toward center front or back and horizontal darts to face downward. Arrange garment with point of dart over rounded end of ironing board to avoid pressing in creases. Insert a strip of brown paper between the dart and the fabric to avoid marking the right side of the fabric.

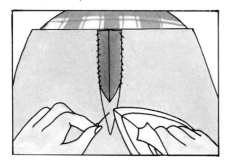

2 On wide or curved darts where the point is pressed flat, use a pin to arrange fabric so that fold of dart lies centered over the stitching line. Use a pressing mit or tailor's ham to shape fabric while pressing curved darts.

Attaching a waistband

A waistband is the simplest way of giving a neat, firm finish to skirt and pants waistlines. A straight waistband is usually made from one piece of fabric which is folded in half lengthwise to form a self-faced band. It should fit snugly, without feeling tight, and be firm enough to withstand strain and allow the garment to hang properly. Attach the waistband when the garment is almost finished, before finishing the hem.

Always stiffen a waistband to give it strength. Either interfacing, grosgrain ribbon (soft or stiffened) or professional waistbanding can be used – which you choose is a matter of personal preference. There are two methods of attaching a waistband. Choose the one appropriate for the type of stiffening you use.

Using interfacing

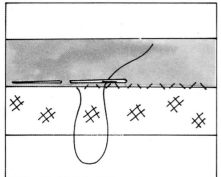

1 *Cut interfacing to half the waistband width. Apply iron-on interfacing by steam pressing in place. Catch stitch sew-in interfacing loosely along the center of the waistband as shown.*

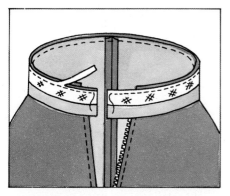

2 *With right sides together, stitch interfaced edge of waistband to waist edge, allowing ⅝in to project at overlap end and 1½in (or amount allowed on pattern) to project on underlap end. With sew-in interfacing, continue stitching to ends of waistband to secure. Trim interfacing close to the stitching line.*

Using waistbanding

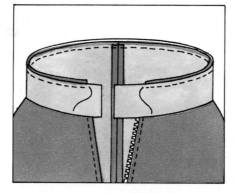

1 *With right sides together, stitch one long edge of waistband to waist edge, allowing ⅝in to project at overlap and 1½ (or amount allowed on pattern) to project at underlap end.*

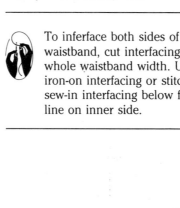

To inferface both sides of waistband, cut interfacing to whole waistband width. Use iron-on interfacing or stitch sew-in interfacing below fold line on inner side.

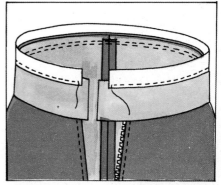

2 *Trim ends of waistbanding ⅝in shorter than waistband at both ends. With lower edge of waistbanding level with first row of stitching, stitch waistbanding to waist seam allowance.*

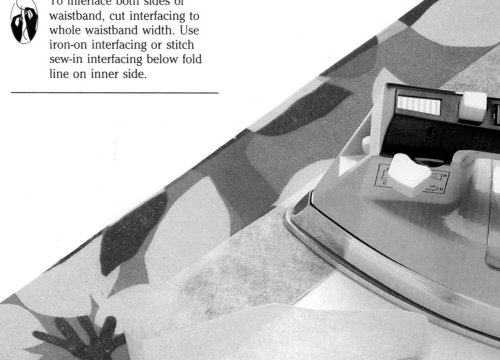

Finishing the waistband

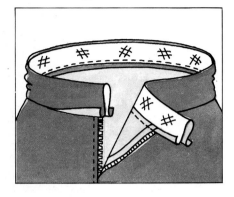

1 *With right sides together, fold waistband in half lengthwise at ends, so top edge of interfacing or waistbanding is level with fold. Turn back seam allowance on loose edge of waistband, so that fold is level with previous line of stitching.*

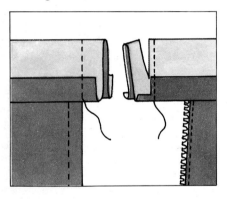

2 *Stitch across ends, ⅝in from raw edges. Stitch across interfacing on interfaced waistband and trim back to stitching. If using waistbanding stitch just outside the ends of stiffening. Trim corners and ends as shown on both versions to reduce bulk and prevent a lumpy finish.*

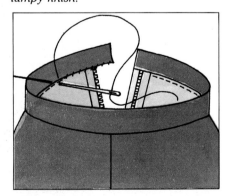

3 *Turn waistband right side out with edge of waistbanding level with fold. Press along fold. Turn seam allowance under along open edge of waistband and catch stitch along previous row of stitching. Press again.*

Waistband stiffenings

There is a good range of different types of stiffenings to choose from, some of which are available in sew-in and iron-on forms, as well as different weights. The following varieties are all suitable for waistbands. Be careful to choose one with the same wash/dry-clean instructions as your fabric.

1 Professional waistbanding is a stiff woven band that does not crease or roll over in wear. It comes in several widths, from ¾ to 2in, and is sewn in as shown on page 35.

2 Stiffened grosgrain ribbon is used in the same way as professional waistbanding. It is available in several widths and colors. Ordinary soft grosgrain ribbon is used instead of a self facing on a waistband made of thick fabric, to reduce bulk.

3 This non-woven iron-on band covers both sides of the waistband. The slots along the center produce a neat fold line.

4 Interfacing is available from the roll in various widths in both sew-in and iron-on forms, and in several weights. Choose interfacing with a fairly firm finish.

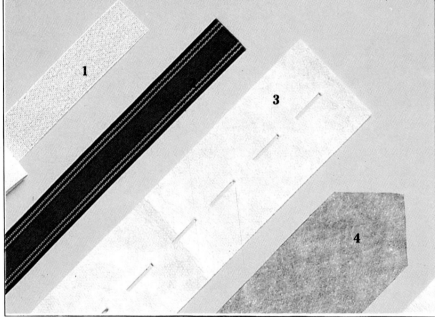

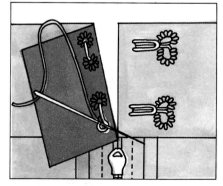

4 *Sew two hooks to wrong side of overlap end, using buttonhole stitch, with ends of hooks about ⅛in from end. Secure top of hook with a couple of stitches. Sew eyes to underlap so they are hidden when waistband is fastened.*

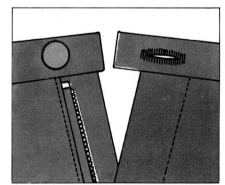

5 *Alternatively, finish with a button. Mark the position of the buttonhole on overlap and work buttonhole by machine or hand. Mark the position of the button beneath the overlap with a pin and sew it in place.*

Gathering

Gathering is a decorative way to provide fullness in a design by drawing up a wide piece of fabric to fit a narrower one. It is an alternative to tucks and pleats and can be used on cuffs, yokes and waistbands. Soft fabrics form attractive gathers whereas stiffer fabrics tend to look bulky, especially on fuller figures. If gathering is for decoration alone, $1\frac{1}{2}$ times the final gathered length is the minimum amount of fabric you need to make convincing gathers, and with sheer fabrics, 3–4 times the final length is required for a really full effect.

Gathering can be done by hand or machine. When stitching by hand, make two rows of small stitches with a knot at one end and a long end at the other. Gathers form more easily if the stitches in the second row fall exactly above those in the first. When stitching by machine, use a longer stitch length than usual, so that you can pull up the fabric without damaging it. Some machines have an attachment to gather fabric onto a straight piece. Practice this on a scrap of your fabric, following the instructions in your manual.

The success of gathering lies in an even distribution of gathers. Keep this evenness with vertically placed pins, and with your fingers as you stitch.

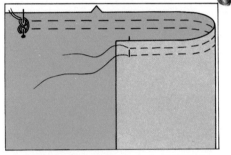

1 *With right side facing, make two rows of stitching ⅛ and ¼in from the seamline. Pull both bobbin threads through to right side at one end and wind around a pin in a figure eight along with the top threads to secure. Repeat with threads at other end.*

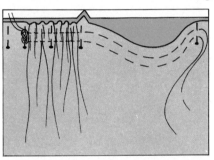

2 *With right sides together, pin gathered piece to straight piece at notches and dots, placing vertically. Pull up both bobbin threads together to fit and secure around a pin. Distribute gathers, pin and baste.*

 If you find it difficult to pull up the gathers, try using a heavier bobbin thread, or loosening the top thread tension.

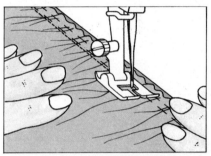

3 *Stitch with the gathered side on top, guiding the gathers carefully to prevent bunching. Press the stitching and then press the seam allowance away from the gathers. Point the tip of the iron into the gathers when pressing to avoid flattening.*

Long lengths

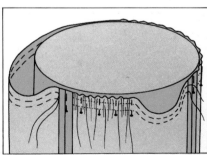

When gathering long lengths, make two rows of stitching as before, but stitch in sections, starting and ending at seams where possible. Pin to straight piece at seams, halfway between seams, notches and dots. Pull up the bobbin threads, gathering half of each section from one end and half from the other.

Shirring

Shirring is another method of gathering, giving soft folds plus all the benefits of using elastic. This makes it particularly suitable for children's clothes and sundresses. It can also be used at the shoulder, waist and hip, as well as on yokes and sleeves. Soft, lightweight fabrics hang best.

Shirring can be worked by hand or machine. Shirring by hand involves making rows of running stitches, but this does not have the flexibility of using elastic or the speed of using the machine. Shirring by machine with an ordinary sewing thread on the top and shirring elastic on the bobbin is by far the easiest and most effective method. Shirring elastic is a core of elastic surrounded by thread and is available in many colors. Choose the color to harmonize or contrast with the fabric. Color can also be added by embroidering over the shirring as a form of mock smocking.

Preparing the fabric

You need 1½ to 3 times the final width of the shirring. The finer the fabric, the greater the width required. Gathers are tighter with a long stitch and more rows. The number of rows you need to stitch depends on where the shirring is used on a garment. Three rows are the minimum required on sleeves, and ten on a bodice, although more rows can be stitched as part of the design. Mark the shirring lines on the right side of the fabric with tailor's chalk, or, if it is easier, guide the side of the presser foot against the previous row of stitching. Fabric normally needs little guiding to sew in a straight line, but after the first row of shirring you will need to hold the fabric flat while you stitch. Take care not to pull the fabric off its straight stitching line at the same time. Read your sewing machine manual too, because there may be a special foot to help center the elastic.

If you want the gathers of shirring without the elasticity, strengthen it by backing with lawn or a spare piece of

your fabric or rows of twill tape. Fabric should cover the panel of shirring from top to bottom, while tape will cover one or two rows at a time. Alternatively, reverse stitch along each row on the wrong side.

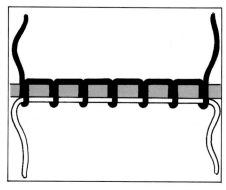

1 *Wind the shirring elastic around the bobbin by hand, under little or no tension. Loosen the top thread tension on the machine to bring the knot just to the underside of the fabric. Experiment on a spare piece of fabric with different stitch lengths. A longer stitch will give a tighter gather. If the shirring is near an edge, finish with a narrow hem before shirring.*

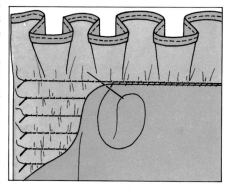

3 *Bring the top threads through to wrong side and knot with elastic. If possible enclose these ends in a seam, otherwise make a small pin tuck to hide the knots and hold them in. To back shirring, place tape or lightweight fabric (with edges pressed under) on wrong side and sew to top and bottom rows.*

 Do not press shirring. The elastic will tighten if you pass it through the steam of a kettle or steam iron (without ironing).

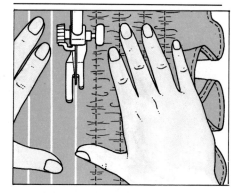

2 *Press the fabric and mark straight lines in chalk on the right side, ⅜-1in apart. If you are stitching on a striped or plaid fabric, follow the lines of the fabric design. Stitch along the first line, leaving long ends. Stitch along remaining lines, stretching the fabric flat as you stitch. Check the width of shirring and pull up the elastic from each side to the required width.*

Zigzag shirring

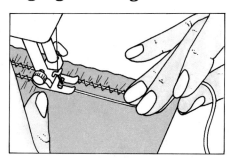

Place a thin, strong cord or shirring elastic on the shirring line and machine stitch over it with a wide zigzag stitch. Take care not to stitch into the cord. Stitch along shirring lines, pulling the elastic as you sew. Pull up cord at the end, taking care not to pull it out. Finish as before.

Pleats

Pleats are an elegant way of controlling fullness, and the result is well worth the time and patience needed. There are several kinds of pleats; some fall in soft folds (unpressed pleats), and others are pressed along the length of the fabric (crisp pleats). Whichever type of pleat you choose to make, the basic principles of marking and folding are the same.

Different types of pleat

A knife pleat is a single fold of fabric pressed to one side. Single knife pleats are normally pressed away from the center front or center back. Knife pleats all around have the folds facing left to right across the back and right to left across the front. They are sometimes shaped $\frac{5}{8}$-$\frac{3}{4}$in wider at the hem to help the hang.

A box pleat is made with the folds of two knife pleats turned away from each other and the underfolds meeting.

An inverted pleat is the reverse of a box pleat, with the folds of two knife pleats meeting at the center. Box and inverted pleats are usually used singly but can be used in series, when they look the same as one another. Where pleats are used in series, hide openings and seams under the pleats as far as possible. Pleats can look bulky, especially on hips, so they are often stitched (and topstitched) to hip level and sometimes lower on inverted pleats. This gives a more flattering line.

The pleats shown here are all made on the grain of the fabric. All pleats should hang folded but without twisting when the garment is worn. Twisted pleats are often caused by accidentally forming the pleats slightly off the grain. Pleats intentionally cut on the bias must be treated slightly differently. Sunray and accordion pleats are commercially made; the names of pleaters can be found in the classified advertisements of magazines. Knife pleating in skirts may also be done commercially. Contact the firms concerned for details of preparation of the fabric for this.

Fabrics

Although any fabric can be pleated, reasonably firm fabrics hold pleats better than soft ones. Fabrics such as worsted, gabardine, linen and firmly woven tweeds and wools are especially good for crisp pleats. Crease-resistant fabrics hold crisp pleats only if they are edgestitched on each fold. Underlined fabrics need extra care in getting the folds of the lining and the top fabric to lie exactly together.

Marking

Different pattern companies mark pleats in different ways. Sometimes the fold line is marked and sometimes only the placement or stitching line, so check which lines you are marking before beginning. Tailor tacking is the best method of marking because the marks are visible on both right and wrong sides of the fabric. Mark and fold the pleats, matching markings, then baste along the fold line. The basting stitches must remain until the garment is completed, in order to support the pleats, which means pressing with the stitches still in place. Use a fine basting thread such as silk to minimize marking the fabric. If basting the folded edge alone does not secure the pleat satisfactorily, baste diagonally across the width of each pleat.

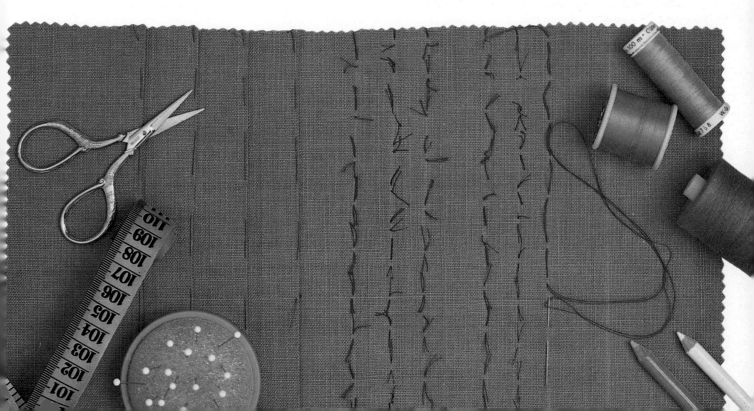

Pressing

Crisp pleats must be steam pressed in place. Support the garment as you press to prevent distortion of the steamed fabric. On thicker fabrics, a towel can be placed under the garment, with the edge of the towel butted up against the fold of the pleat, to give an even thickness. This is sometimes a more effective way of preventing ridges than using brown paper.

Stitching

Fit and alter if necessary before stitching. Pleats may need to overlap a little at the waist to fit, leaving the full pleated width at the hips. Stitch, press in the right direction, hem and then topstitch and/or edgestitch.

Making the pleats

Lay out the garment piece on a large flat surface and tailor tack along the fold lines. Then, using a different color thread, tailor tack along the pleat placement or stitching lines. Accuracy here is important for the correct hang of the pleats. Remove pattern piece carefully.

Stitched inverted pleat

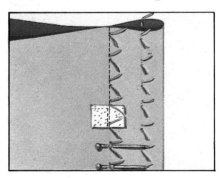

With right side inside, bring the fold lines and stitching lines together. Pin (and baste) along the stitching line. Stitch to required detpth, strengthening with interfacing (optional). Machine baste along remaining stitching line. Fold on fold lines and press in place.

Topstitching

Topstitching is a decorative finish and emphasizes the flattering vertical line of a pleat. It also holds the pleat in place and helps it to hang smoothly. Diagonal stitching at the bottom of the stitching or topstitching lines reduces stress on the fabric at these points. A square of iron-on interfacing can also be applied at these points to strengthen. Apply at the turn of the stitching on a knife pleat and the base of the stitching on an inverted pleat. Arrowheads and bar tacks made on the right side at these points are other decorative ways of easing the strain.

Edgestitching

Edgestitching may be done on the underfolds only, or the top folds only, or both. This ensures that the folds stay in place. The hem must be made before edgestitching, but waistband or other garment pieces added afterward.

Unpressed pleats

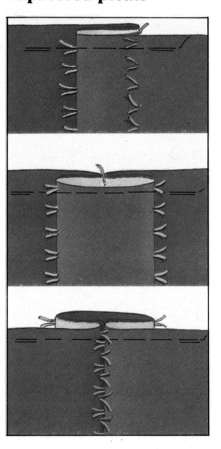

These are often marked only for one or two inches from the top of the garment. Fold the fabric wrong sides together on the fold line and bring placement lines together. Bring fold to one side for a knife pleat or both sides for a box or inverted pleat and baste across the top.

Stitched knife pleat

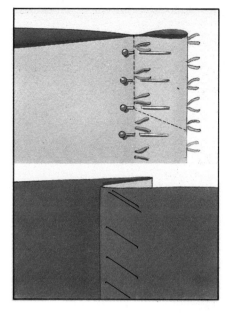

Fold fabric right sides together on fold line and bring stitching lines together. Pin and baste for fitting. Stitch to the required depth, pivot fabric and stitch to fold line as shown. For crisp pleats, machine baste along remaining stitching line. Baste and press in the desired direction.

Pressing

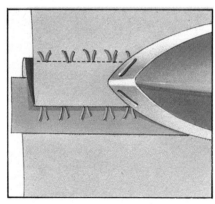

Steam press crisp pleats on right side using press cloth, and then on wrong side. Support the whole garment so the fabric does not lose its shape by hanging over the edge of the board. If pressing on wrong side produces ridges on right side, place strips of brown paper under each fold.

 When folding and pinning the pleats, work on a large table or an ironing board that is long enough to take the full length of the pleat.

Topstitching

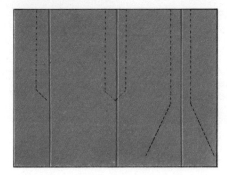

With the right side uppermost, stitch through all thicknesses to the point where the pleat is released, ⅛-¼in from the fold. The pleat is given added support by slanting the stitching at the bottom. Take thread ends through to wrong side and fasten off.

Hems

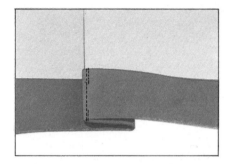

Hem the garment as usual but always hem before edgestitching. Consider edgestitching the underfold(s) the depth of the hem alone. If the pleats sag a little on the underfolds, make the inside hemline a little higher than the outside hemline so they do not show.

Edgestitching

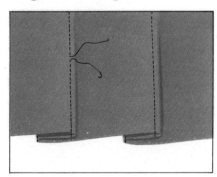

After fitting and checking the hang of the pleats, stitch along the fold of the pleats beginning at the bottom. If pleats are topstitched, topstitch first, then edgestitch to the topstitching at the same distance from the fold. Bring thread ends through to wrong side and knot.

41

Casings

Casings are created to take a drawstring or elastic and provide another means of gathering. Elastic gives a snug fit, while drawstrings have the asset of adjustability. Both are often used at necklines, waists and sleeve edges. A casing can be made by folding over the edge of the garment and stiching to make a channel (a folded casing), or by stitching a separate strip of fabric to the garment (an applied casing). They are always machine stitched for strength. Place pins at right angles to the length of the casing and with practice you can stitch without basting. Avoid stretching bias tape as you pin, or you will make it narrower. Trim seam allowances to $\frac{1}{4}$in under a casing to reduce bulk.

Casing strips

Purchased bias binding (available in several widths) is ideal for curved hems or applied casings. You can also use strips of your fabric, if it is lightweight, or of lining fabric, cut on the true bias and joined to be a little longer than the finished casing. If the casing line is on the grain of the fabric, the casing may also be cut on the grain. Remember to add a minimum of $\frac{1}{4}$in seam allowance to each side of the casing when cutting out, and press to wrong side before you begin. Wider elastic may also be thicker, and the casing should be cut up to $\frac{1}{4}$in wider than the width of the elastic to allow for this.

Headings

A heading on a folded casing forms a decorative ruffle in double thickness fabric. A similar effect (and a good alternative for thicker fabrics) can be made by stitching a narrow hem along the top of the heading and applying a casing the depth of the heading from it.

Openings

The type of opening you choose to make will depend on the type of casing which is being used and also on whether you are using elastic or a drawstring. Openings for drawstrings are made on the main piece of the garment before the casing is applied. All other openings are made on the casing.

Straight edge casing

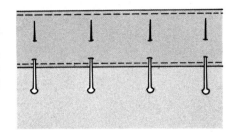

Press under $\frac{1}{4}$in on the raw edge, then turn under the depth of the casing. This depth is the width of the elastic plus $\frac{1}{8}$-$\frac{1}{4}$in, depending on the thickness. Pin in place. Decide on a suitable opening and stitch along the lower folded edge of the casing. Stitch close to top fold (optional).

Casing with heading

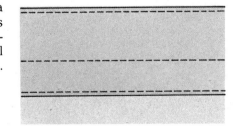

Press under $\frac{1}{4}$in on the raw edge, then turn under the depth of the casing plus the heading. Pin and stitch along lower folded edge, leaving an opening at a suitable point. Mark the depth of the casing from lower edge in chalk and stitch. Stitch close to top fold (optional) to give a firm edge.

 On thick fabrics, mark the fold lines for casings by stitching with a long machine stitch. This makes it easy to press the folds accurately. Remove threads before machine stitching casing.

Curved edge casing

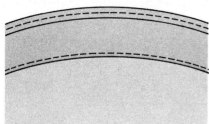

Cut a bias strip slightly longer than the edge, and the width of the casing (and heading, if appropriate), plus ¼ in seam allowances. Place raw edges of binding and fabric right sides together and stitch ¼ in from edge. Press casing to wrong side. Stitch lower edge and top folded edge (optional) and upper casing line if there is a heading.

Opening at an edge

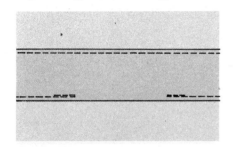

Stitch the edge of the casing, leaving an opening equal to twice the width of the elastic (½-2in). Begin and finish stitching with two to three reverse stitches. After threading elastic, stitch across the gap. The stitching is less bulky if all the threads are taken through to the wrong side and knotted, rather than reverse stitched.

Applied casing opening

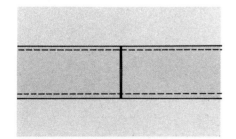

Turn under at least ¼ in on one end and pin the casing in place. Cut the other end of the binding ¼ in longer than the edge and turn under. Align the ends and stitch the casing without breaking the stitching where the ends meet. Thread the casing, then slipstitch the opening closed.

Applied casing

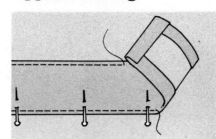

Turn under seam allowances on both long edges of a straight or bias strip, leaving it the width of the casing. Center the binding on the fabric, wrong sides together. Pin and stitch close to both edges, leaving an opening as appropriate. If the casing is near an edge, finish the edge with a narrow hem before applying the casing.

Opening in a seam

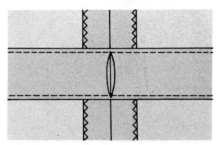

Stitch the casing along both edges and cut the stitching of a seam that crosses it. Take care not to cut the fabric. After threading with elastic, close the opening by slipstitching. The same method can be used on the right side of the fabric for a drawstring, but the opening is made before the casing is applied and the ends sewn in to fasten securely.

Drawstring opening

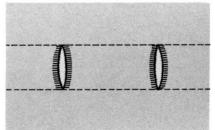

Before applying the casing, make two slits the width of the casing on the right side of the fabric, one each side of the point at which the string will tie. Work around slits in buttonhole stitch. Apply casing to the wrong side and thread the drawstring in and out of buttonholes with a safety pin.

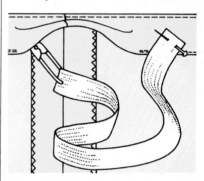
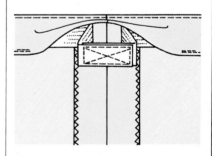

Ruffles and flounces

Ruffles are easy to make and add a touch of femininity to the plainest of clothes. They can be made and attached in various ways to give different results.

Straight ruffles are made from strips of fabric gathered along one side and let into a seam or joined to a flat edge. They may be cut on the straight grain or on the bias, as a single layer with a hem at the outer edge, or as a double layer with the raw edges stitched into the seam. Double layer ruffles are only suitable for lightweight and fine fabrics which gather easily.

Precious antique lace or eyelet lace with one decorative edge can make a very attractive detachable ruffle. Bind the gathered edge and then catch in place just beneath the garment edge.

Ruffles can also be applied to the outside of a garment, to make a hemline flounce or a shirt-front ruffle. These must be finished on both edges.

Fabrics
Most materials used for dresses and blouses are suitable for ruffles, provided they can be gathered successfully. Gingham, lawn, organdy, voile, taffeta, poplin and lightweight wools are all good possibilities.

Calculating amounts
The amount to allow for gathering ruffles depends on the weight and thickness of the fabric being used. If possible, experiment first with a sample strip of fabric cut to the desired depth and at least 12in long. Make a note of the exact length, then gather along one long edge and draw up until the correct amount of fullness is obtained. Secure the thread and measure along the gathered edge. If it has been reduced by half you will need to cut the strip twice the length of the edge it is to join, plus extra for seaming. You may need less than twice the length for gathering a thick fabric, and as much as three times the length for very fine fabrics.

The finished depth of the ruffle can be anything from a narrow edging of about ¾in to a generous hem flounce of 9in. Decide on the appropriate depth for the garment and add extra for seams, headings and hems, according to the type of ruffle being made.

Cutting out
For a single layer ruffle cut strips of fabric of the required depth plus hem and seam allowances and join to make the required length. If appropriate to the design, join the last two short edges to form a ring.

For a double layer ruffle, cut strips to twice the desired finished depth, plus 1¼in for seam allowances, and join to make the required length.

When making a detachable collar from lace or a similar material with one decorative edge, cut the unfinished edge to the required depth, allowing ⅜in seam allowance.

For an outside stitched hem flounce, cut strips of the required depth plus hem allowances on both edges and enough for the heading ruffle. Join strips to make the required length.

Cut a single ruffle with two finished edges to the required width and length plus ¾in for narrow hems (unless using a purchased trim with two finished edges, in which case allow hems at each end only).

Hems
Outer edges of single layer ruffles may be edge-stitched by machine, decoratively zigzagged or shell edged. Alternatively, slipstitch or roll-hem the edges by hand.

Single layer ruffle stitched to an edge

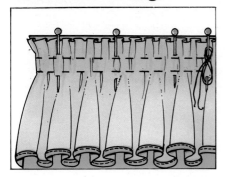

Stitch a narrow hem along one long edge and press. Gather opposite edge, draw up evenly and pin, baste and stitch to garment edge, right sides together. Trim and finish raw edges together. Press seam away from ruffle.

Double layer ruffle enclosed in a seam

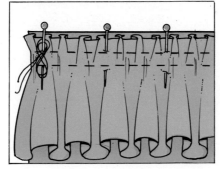

1 Fold ruffle piece in half lengthwise, wrong sides together, and press. Run gathering threads through both layers at raw edge, draw up evenly and pin to right side of one garment piece with raw edges even.

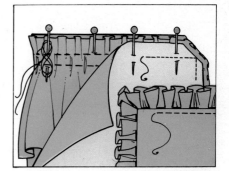

2 Place other garment piece face down on ruffle with raw edges even. Pin, baste and stitch along seamline, If seam is exposed, trim and finish raw edges together. If it is enclosed in a facing, trim seam and corners, baste through all layers at edge and press.

Detachable ruffle

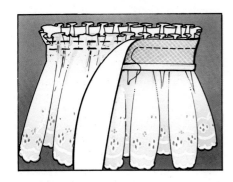

1 Gather unfinished edge and draw up to desired length. Fasten off. Cut bias strip of fabric 1½in wide by length required plus seam allowances. Press ⅜in to wrong side along one edge. With right sides together, stitch other edge to gathered ruffle, taking ⅜in seam.

2 Trim gathered edge of ruffle back to ⅜in if necessary, tuck in at each end of binding and turn folded edge of binding over to wrong side of ruffle. Slipstitch binding in place by hand, or machine stitch along previous stitching line.

Single ruffle with two finished edges

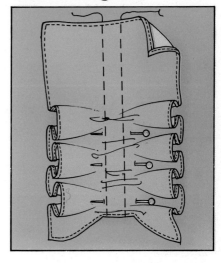

Mark center of ruffle strip. Stitch narrow hems all around edge and press. Make parallel rows of gathering on each side of center line and draw up to desired size. Pin, baste and topstitch alongside gathering threads.

Two rows of gathering are easier to control than one. Make two parallel rows of stitching within the seam allowance, or stitch ⅛in to each side of the stitching line and remove the visible gathering thread when stitching is complete. Use the longest stitch length and slacken upper thread tension.

Outside hemline flounce

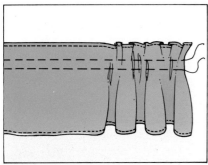

1 Stitch narrow hems along both edges of ruffle piece and press. Baste along stitching line at desired depth from one edge to allow for heading and gather on each side of this line. Remove basting and draw up gathering threads.

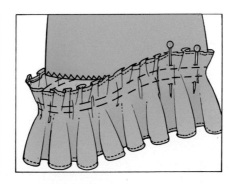

2 Check hem level and garment length and finish edge of main garment piece. Place gathered edge of flounce on garment, right sides upward; pin, baste and stitch between gathering threads. Remove previous stitching.

45

Tucks

Tucks will always be a popular fashion design feature on garments such as dresses, blouses, children's wear and lingerie. Tucks are machine or hand-stitched folds of fabric made on the straight grain on the right side of the fabric. They can be used for a decorative effect or to hold fullness in place and give shaping. If tucks are part of a pattern design, the pattern will indicate the width and spacing between the tucks. However, if you are designing your own tucking as a decorative part of a design, you will have to determine the width of tuck you want and space them yourself.

Tucks can be used in groups or clusters and in graduated widths. The width can vary from $\frac{3}{4}$in to tiny pin tucks of about $\frac{1}{8}$in for use on small areas. They can be made the full length of the section of garment being tucked or they can be stitched part of the way down to give fullness below.

Where possible, or if adding tucks to your design, stitch the tucks first and then lay the paper pattern piece over them and cut out in the usual way. This will be easier since you can work with a straight piece of fabric.

Estimating fabric amounts
If you are designing your own tucking, first decide where the tucks should be placed on the figure, then how wide and how far apart you want them. Having done this you can then estimate how much extra fabric you will require for the tucking. If tucks and spacing are equal, you will need twice the finished width of fabric. If the fold of the tuck touches the stitching of the previous tuck, as in a blind tuck, three times the finished width is required.

Marking the tucks
Tucks are usually made on the lengthwise grain of the fabric, as it is always firmer than the crosswise grain and gives a better finish. Transfer the position of the tucks from pattern to fabric using a tracing wheel and dressmaker's carbon paper or a chalk pencil. Tailor's chalk and tacks do not provide such accurate, sharp lines.

Where the position of the tucks is not indicated on the pattern, or you are designing your own, use a gauge to aid measuring and make each tuck in turn as you work across the width of the fabric (see Helping Hand).

Stitching the tucks
Always stitch tucks so that the upper thread of the stitching will be visible when the garment is worn. When tucks are used on both right and left sides of a garment, they are turned and pressed in opposite directions from the center and you must alternate the direction of the stitching on the tucks on both right and left sides to prevent the tucked section from twisting.

As tucks are topstitched they require a shorter stitch length. The thread should either blend perfectly with the fabric color or be a definite contrast.

Pin tucks
There are several methods of tucking, depending on the effect you require. The most popular form of tucking is pin tucking. Pin tucks are small fine tucks usually found in sheer blouses, lingerie, childen's wear and garments made of fine or lightweight fabric. As they are so small, basting is almost impossible, so after marking the tuck lines, fold the fabric with tuck lines matching and stitch, holding fabric firmly and stitching slowly. Pin tucks can be made on most fabrics, whereas wider tucks should only be made on fabric which can take a sharp crease.

Pressing
First press the stitching on the wrong side of each tuck with the point of the iron to embed the stitching. Then, using a press cloth on the wrong side, press the tucks to one side, flat against the fabric. Work a line of staystitching along top and bottom edge of tucks to hold in place.

 Before making the tucks on your garment, make a few practice tucks in a scrap of your fabric to be certain that the stitch length, tuck size and spacing are correct.

Making wide tucks

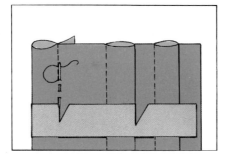

Starting at the right-hand edge, crease or press the fabric along the fold lines, matching markings or using a gauge as a guide. Keep the creases on the straight grain. Baste, then machine stitch the tucks or hand sew with a fine running stitch. Sometimes the fold line may be marked by pulling out a thread.

Making pin tucks

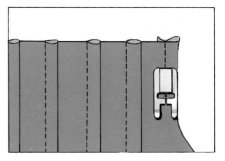

Mark the position of each tuck. With tuck lines matching, fold the tuck wrong sides together and stitch slowly close to the folded edge. Press. If stitching by hand, use a long slender needle, fine thread and a very small running stitch. Press tucks flat.

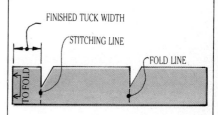
Making a gauge

FINISHED TUCK WIDTH

STITCHING LINE

FOLD LINE

TO FOLD

Make the gauge by cutting a strip of heavy cardboard long enough to measure the width of several tucks and spaces. Mark the finished width of the tuck by cutting a notch in the cardboard the tuck width away from the left-hand edge. Make a second notch the finished tuck width plus space between stitching lines from the straight edge of the first notch.

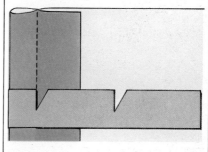

Working from right to left across the fabric, make the first tuck at the desired position, using the distance between the left-hand edge of the gauge and the first notch as a guide. Baste and press tuck to the right.

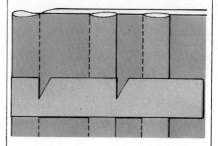

Make the next tuck by aligning the straight edge of the second notch with the fold of the first tuck and folding the fabric at the left-hand edge of the gauge. The straight edge of the first notch marks the stitching line. Baste, moving the gauge along the length of the tuck as you stitch. Continue folding and basting, aligning the gauge in the same way to make regular tucks.

Cutting out

When the tucks extend only a few inches into the garment section, and are then creased, pull the threads to the wrong side and finish with a knot.

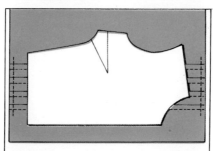

If an entire section of a garment such as a pocket, yoke or blouse front is to be tucked, it is easier to tuck the fabric first and then cut out the section according to the pattern. Make the tucks as shown opposite and press. Place the paper pattern over the tucked fabric and cut out in the usual way.

Neck facings

Facings are the simplest way to finish neck edges. The most common type are folded over to the inside of a garment to give a neat plain finish with the facing invisible from the right side. The secret of this type of facing is that it should be invisible. Pay special attention to stitching the neckline in a smooth even line, and most important of all, trim and clip the seam allowance well so the facing will lie flat. Understitching will help enormously by preventing the neck seam from rolling back; it also makes it unnecessary to catch stitch the outer edge of the facing to the garment, which often shows an ugly stitch line no matter how carefully you do it.

Interfacing

First choose your interfacing carefully. Pick a fairly soft one, as it does not need to stiffen the neckline but just give a fraction extra body to prevent the neckline from stretching.

Apply the interfacing to the wrong side of the facing pieces. If using an iron-on type, steam press in place with a damp cloth so the steam is evenly dispersed all over to activate the adhesive evenly. Just press downward without running the iron to and fro, which can move the interfacing about, making wrinkles. With sew-in interfacing, pin it to the pieces with pins at right angles to the edges and treat interfacing and fabric as one.

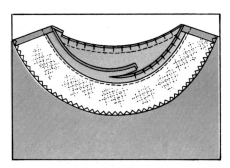

1 *Trim seam allowance on sew-in interfacing right back to stitching. Trim fabric seam allowance to about ¼in. On curves clip seam allowance almost to stitching about every ⅝in and even closer on tight curves.*

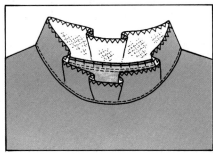

2 *Turn and press facing up onto seam allowance, pushing the iron from the garment toward the facing to open the seam right out. Understitch by stitching through facing and seam allowances only, just above neck seams.*

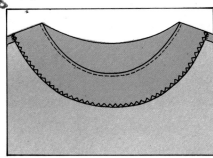

3 *Fold facing over to the inside. The understitching should help the seam to roll over naturally to just inside the neckline. Press, then catch stitch edge of facing to shoulder seam allowance.*

Making the facing

Stitch front facing to back facing across the shoulder seam. Trim seams to about $\frac{1}{4}$ in and press open. Finish outer edge of facing with zigzag stitch or three step zigzag (tricot). Press edge. Non-fray fabrics can be left raw or trimmed with pinking shears.

Stitching

With right sides together stitch facing around neck edge. Watch the edge of the presser foot to keep it evenly spaced from the raw edge, so keeping the stitching smoothly in line. On curves, keep the needle point and front edge of the foot parallel with the raw edge, as this is where you are stitching and are about to stitch.

Decorative neck facings

Decorative facings finish on the right side of the garment to give a special style feature. They may be in a contrasting fabric, or use the pattern of the fabric in a different direction from the main part of the garment. Trimmings add a special touch when inserted in the neckline seam or under the outer edge of a facing. Decorative facings are made in the same way as concealed facings but are stitched with the right side of the facing to the wrong side of the garment to fold over to the right side when finished. The seam allowances are understitched to the garment rather than the facing. Instead of finishing the outer edge of the facing, leave it till last, then tuck under the raw edge and baste and topstitch to the garment from the right side, stitching through any trimmings to secure them.

Outer edge trim on decorative facing

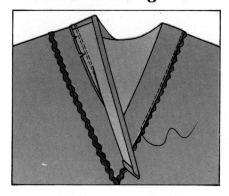

Trim outer edge of a decorative right side facing with lace, cording or rickrack by inserting the trim under the folded outer edge of the facing and topstitching in place.

Decorative facing cut on the bias

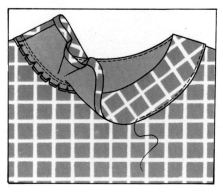

Change the grain line arrow on pattern to run at 45° to original grain line. Stitch facing to neck with right side of facing to wrong side of garment and turn over to the right side.

Decorative facing featuring stripes

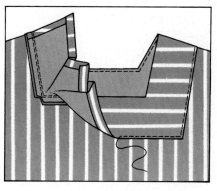

Cut facing with stripes running in opposite direction to those on garment. On square facings clip corners of seam allowance almost to stitching before understitching to garment.

Neckline trim on concealed facing

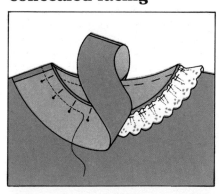

Add braid, lace or cording to a concealed facing by inserting it between garment and facing with the right side of the trim facing the garment. Baste the trim in place, then baste the facing in place and stitch through all layers.

Front facings

Front facings are a neat way of finishing the front edge of a garment. They can be cut as one with the front piece as an attached facing, or cut as a separate piece. Separate facings are normally attached to the right side, then turned to the wrong side and caught down. They are usually cut from self fabric, but if the main fabric is particularly bulky, it is possible to substitute lining or fabric of a lighter weight for hidden facings.

The alternative to an ordinary faced edge is a facing band which is attached to the wrong side and then brought over to the right side as a decorative feature. It can be applied to the upper (buttonholed) front only, with a hidden front facing on the underside. This is ideal for a blouse or dress with a shirt-style collar which extends to the extreme front edges of the garment. If made in checks, stripes or a textured weave, the band can look interesting cut on the bias.

Interfacing

Interfacing gives a crisp edge to the garment fronts. Always apply iron-on interfacing to the wrong side of the facing pieces only. Sew-in interfacing may be attached to the wrong side of the garment or to the facing pieces.

Preparing the facing

Before attaching the facing, stitch, press and finish the main seams of the garment. If the pattern specifies a neckline facing, join this to the front facing pieces and then press the seams open. Finish the outer edge of the facing by zigzag stitching, overcasting or edge-stitching.

Front band facing

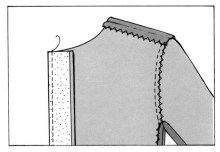

1 *Cut a strip of fabric the length of front edge by desired width, plus 1¼in for seams. Cut interfacing ⅝in narrower and apply to wrong side, leaving ⅝in margin at one side. With right side of band to wrong side of garment, stitch interfaced edge to right front.*

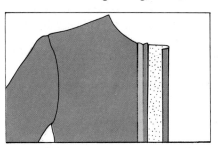

2 *Press seam as stitched and then open out band and press seam open with the tip of the iron only. Fold ⅝in to wrong side along outer edge of band and press to hold in place.*

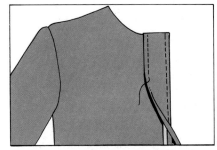

3 *Bring band over to right side of garment and baste both edges through all thicknesses, making sure band is an even width along its length. Topstitch ⅜in in from each edge and remove basting. Make vertical buttonholes.*

Separate front facing

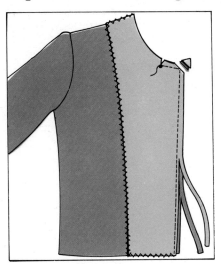

1 *Place facing pieces on fronts, with right sides together, edges even and notches matching. Stitch along edge to points indicated at neck edge. Trim facing seam allowance to ¼in and garment seam allowance to ⅜in, and clip corners close to stitching.*

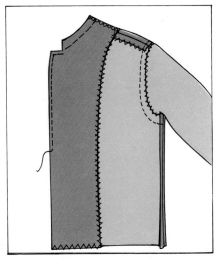

2 *Turn facing over to inside and carefully push out corner from inside using the point of a knitting needle. Baste through outer edge, rolling the seam between finger and thumb to bring it to the edge. Press and catch loose outer edge of facing to seam allowances with herringbone stitch.*

Combined facings

Combined facings are used on sleeveless styles where it is neater and simpler to combine the neck facing with the armhole facing in one piece. As the facing is stitched to both armhole and neck it is not possible to turn the facing over in the usual way. Instead, the facing is applied before the shoulder seam is stitched, and the shoulders are turned out through the facing. With this type of facing it is important to take very accurate seam allowances around the shoulder area.

Interfacing
Combined facings tend to be deeper than ordinary facings, and as they include the armhole facing it is not usual to interface them. However, if the fabric is loosely woven and there is a danger of the neckline stretching, interface the neck area only. Trim the interfacing so it covers an area about 2in deep around the neckline, leaving the rest of the combined facing free of interfacing.

Shoulder fastening styles
Styles that fasten at the shoulder are very simple to finish with a combined facing. The facing is stitched in place with one continuous row of stitching around armhole, neck and shoulder straps. After trimming, the straps are turned right side out and the facing over to the inside with all raw edges neatly enclosed. This is a good style for growing girls as it is easy to allow for growth. Simply lengthen front straps on front and front facing so they underlap farther under back straps, and move the buttons as required.

Understitching
It is impossible to understitch combined facings all around. However the finish is greatly improved by understitching the front and back neck and lower part of the armhole for as far as possible. The inaccessible shoulder part of the facing is already held by stitching at neck and armhole which will prevent the seam from rolling back.

Preparing combined facing
With right sides together and raw edges even, stitch front facing to back facing at side seams. Trim the seam allowance to half width and press seam open. Zigzag stitch around lower edge of facing to finish. Press seam allowance to wrong side along all shoulder edges. Trim this pressed seam allowance to about $\frac{1}{4}$in, before stitching facing to garment.

Facing with shoulder seam

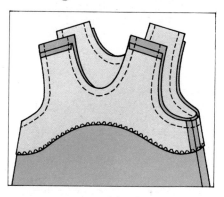 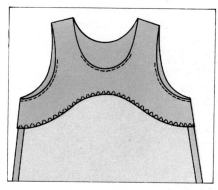

1 *With shoulder seam allowances on facing pressed to wrong side, place facing and garment right sides together and stitch around neck and armhole edges. Press seams as stitched. Trim seam allowance and clip on curves. Turn straps through the facing so they are right side out.*

2 *Press facing up onto the seam allowance, pushing iron from garment to facing. Understitch neck and lower armhole seams by machine stitching through facing and seam allowance only, just above the seam. Turn facing to inside and press.*

Facing with shoulder fastening

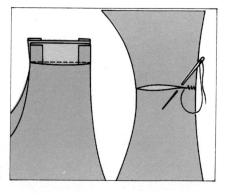 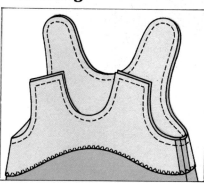

3 *With right sides together, stitch garment shoulder seams, taking care not to catch pressed shoulder edge of facing as you stitch. Trim seam and press open. Tuck in seam allowance and slipstitch pressed edges of facing together to cover seam.*

On a combined facing with shoulder fastenings, stitch facing to garment around all neck, shoulder and armhole edges. Trim and clip seam allowance and turn right side out. understitch neck and lower armhole as before.

SLEEVES, COLLARS AND POCKETS
Faced slit openings

Faced slit openings can be used at necklines or on long sleeves. Plain facings are used on wrist openings and are also suitable for center back neck openings. Combined neck/slit facings are a good way of finishing center front openings and are applied in a similar way. The slit needs to be at least 3in long on sleeves and 6in long on a bodice to allow for getting the garment on and off without straining the opening.

Preparing the facing
Mark the slash and stitching lines carefully on the wrong side of the garment before removing pattern tissue. Always cut plain facings and combined neck/slit facings with the straight grain parallel to the slit marking. Finish the raw edges of the facing by turning under and stitching or zigzag stitching.

Decorative right side facing
As with other types of facing, the right side of the facing can be stitched to the wrong side of the garment and turned to the right side to make a decorative right side facing (see page 49). Press the raw edges of the facing to the wrong side before stitching the facing in place and then topstitch to the right side.

Slit opening in a seam
Where the slit is part of a seam, mark the length of the slit and increase the width of the seam allowances on each side. Allow 1in seam allowance on a sleeve and 2in on a bodice. Stitch the seam to the bottom of the slit, finish seam allowances to top of slit and press seam open to form slit opening.

 Strengthen the point by applying iron-on interfacing to the facing and reducing the stitch length near the point. The interfacing will also help to hold the finished shape of the opening.

Sleeve openings

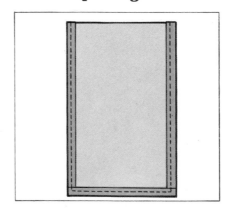

1 *Cut a strip of self fabric on the straight grain, 3in wide and 2in longer than the finished opening. Apply a strip of lightweight iron-on interfacing to the wrong side (optional). Finish both long and one short edge. With right sides together, pin the facing to the garment, aligning both raw edges, and the center of the facing with the marking for the slit.*

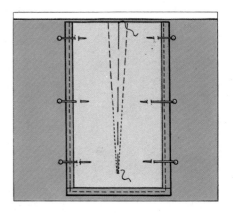

2 *Baste facing to garment along slash line, showing the exact length of the opening. beginning at raw edge, stitch along stitching line toward the point. Reduce stitch length near the point, pivot the fabric at the base of the opening and make one stitch across the end to make turning to wrong side easier. Continue along other side, increasing stitch length again, to raw edge.*

3 *Press, then cut along the marking almost to stitching at the base of the opening. Turn the facing to the wrong side, rolling the fabric in your fingers to bring the seam exactly to the edge. Baste close to edge and press in place. Slipstitch the finished edge of facing to garment to prevent fabric from rolling out at point.*

Neckline openings

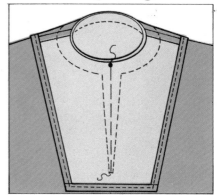

Cut a combined neck/slit facing and join to back neck facing across shoulder seams. Pin, baste and stitch the facing to the garment around neck edge and opening as above. Trim, grade and clip the neckline curves, cut along slash line and turn facings to wrong side. Press and catch the facing to shoulder seams using herringbone stitch.

Setting in a sleeve

The set-in sleeve is a shaped sleeve which is eased or gathered over the shoulder before being inserted into the armhole. The height and curve of the sleeve cap gives room for movement on the shoulder, while the underarm at the front of the sleeve is scooped out more than at the back to prevent excess bunching of fabric. This sleeve curve must also be eased to the different armhole curve.

Easing in a sleeve

The pattern markings will indicate which section of the sleeve cap requires easestitching, by means of circles, notches, or sometimes both. It is customary to use one notch at the front of the sleeve and a double one at the back. On row of easestitching may be enough, but two are a precaution against broken threads or strained fabric. Remember to leave long thread ends for pulling up.

Since it is easier to work on smaller areas of fabric, the sleeves must be formed before being inserted. Join the sleeve seam, then pin and baste the sleeves into the armholes to check the hang and the length. Alter if necessary. When pinning into the armhole, make sure you match the stitching lines at the underarm, and the notch or dot at the center of the sleeve cap with the shoulder seam. Always pin, baste and stitch with the sleeve uppermost to ensure a smooth seam.

Test the effects of heat and steam on a spare piece of fabric before you begin. Some fabrics shrink easily, others hardly at all, and some retain steam marks. Although it is quicker to set in a sleeve without shrinking out the fullness, sometimes fabric is difficult and is helped by shaping beforehand. If you do not press out the fullness in the seam allowance before stitching, you must do so afterward.

A few fabrics (such as velveteen and vinyls) cannot be eased and a few fabrics are too heavy or bulky. These fabrics require special attention and often the pattern has to be adjusted to remove some of the ease. Two-piece sleeves and sleeves with gathered caps can be inserted in the same way, with dots to match with the underarm seam and intentional tucks respectively.

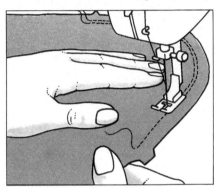

1 *Set the machine to a long stitch length and make two rows of easestitching between the notches on the wrong side of the fabric. Stitch within the seam allowance, ⅛in and ¼in from the seamline. Join the sleeve seam, press open and finish. Check the hang and length of the sleeve and finish with a hem or cuff.*

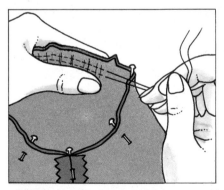

3 *Turn sleeve right side out and thread through armhole so right sides are together. Working from the inside of the sleeve, pin at right angles to the seamline, matching underarm seams, notches and dots. Adjust the ease, making sure it is evenly distributed, and pin at ½in intervals, with raw edges together. Baste close to the seamline, using even basting stitches. Check to make sure the sleeve lies smoothly.*

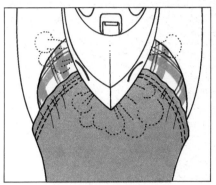

2 *Pull up the threads as required and wind ends around pins to fasten. Distribute the fullness equally, leaving a flat area ½in to each side of the shoulder seam mark, where the grain does not allow easing. Place the sleeve head over a tailor's ham or a rolled towel at the end of your ironing board and steam press the fullness, gently easing it into the fabric.*

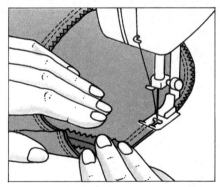

4 *With the sleeve on top, stitch the seam, beginning at the underarm. Stitch again ¼in from the seamline and trim close to stitching. Unless the sleeve is to be lined, finish raw edges together using zigzag stitch. The seam can be trimmed below the notches only, to give a little padding above. Steam press out the fullness if you have not already done so, and turn the seam toward the sleeve.*

Inserting a raglan sleeve

The raglan sleeve is a variation of the set-in sleeve but fits into a deeper or an irregularly shaped armhole. The sleeve can be cut in one piece with a shoulder dart to give shaping over the shoulder line, or it can be cut in two pieces with the seamline down the center of the sleeve and the shaping for the shoulder line going into this seam. This shaping is not needed on designs where the raglan sleeve and bodices are gathered onto a bound neckline .

As with the set-in sleeve, ease is allowed on the sleeve seams and the sleeve section will require easing when it is joined to the back and front bodice pieces. However, there is not enough ease to required a gathering thread.

The raglan sleeve is used a great deal in children's wear, sportswear and outer garments such as coats and raincoats.

Fitting the sleeve

Transfer all markings on the sleeve and armhole accurately from the pattern to the fabric. Always pin, baste and fit the sleeve before stitching it in place. The shoulder length and fit of the shoulder dart or seam along the shoulder are very important. The dart may require lengthening or shortening, depending on whether you have broad or narrow shoulders, and the curve of the seamline over the shoulder may also need adjusting. A shoulder dart in this position will need to be slashed down the center fold and pressed open. When pressing a shoulder dart or seam at the shoulder, always use a pressing mitt or tailor's ham. If you have neither these, use a small towel rolled into a mitt.

Stitching the sleeve

The sleeve can be stitched to the front and back bodice pieces before stitching the underarm and side seams in one continuous seam. Alternatively, the underarm and side seams can be stitched separately, and the sleeve stitched into the armhole afterward. It is generally easier to stitch the sleeve to the bodice first, especially if working on a small armhole, as in children's wear.

 Staystitch the armhole, shoulder and neck edges of the sleeve $\frac{1}{8}$in from stitching line, to prevent stretching.

Stitching the sleeve

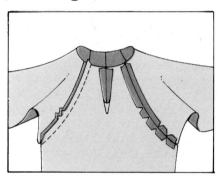

1 *With right sides together and notches matching, pin sleeve to bodice front and back, easing in sleeve fullness by pinning at right angles to the seam. Baste and stitch. Clip seam allowances at armhole curve and along sleeve seam allowance only. Finish and press open.*

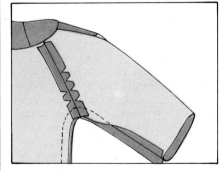

2 *With right sides together and armhole seams matching at underarm, pin and baste the underarm seam of sleeve and the side of bodice and stitch in one continuous seam. Finish raw edges and press seam open.*

Preparing the sleeve

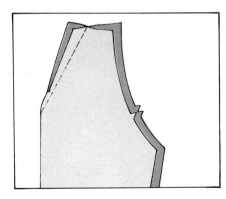

On a one-piece raglan sleeve with shoulder dart, fold right sides together, matching markings, and pin, baste and stitch the shoulder dart from the neck edge to the point. Secure ends of thread. Slash dart almost to point, finish raw edges and press open.

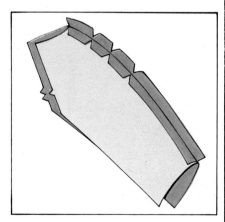

On a two-piece raglan sleeve with shoulder seam, place right sides together, matching notches, and pin, baste and stitch the shoulder and sleeve seam. Clip the seam allowances over the shoulder to allow them to lie flat. Finish and press seam open.

Alternative method

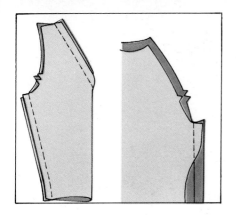

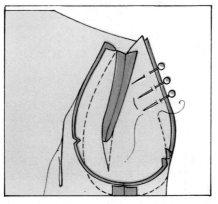

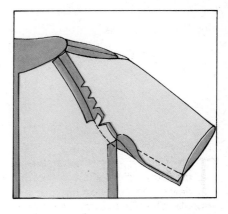

1 *Prepare shoulder dart or seam. With right sides together and notches matching, pin, baste and stitch underarm sleeve seam and bodice side seam. Finish and press seams open.*

2 *Turn sleeve right side out and pin to front and back bodice pieces right sides together, matching notches and underarm seams. Baste. Stitch from one neck edge to the other.*

3 *Clip seam allowance at underarm curve and along the sleeve seam allowance only. Finish and press seam open from neckline to the armhole curve. Press seam around underarm curve toward the sleeve.*

HELPING HAND

Stripes and plaids

Whether you are working with stripes or plaids, it is important to arrange the pattern pieces on the fabric so that the lines of the pattern are balanced on the garment pieces and match at the seamlines for a really professional finish. The following method is a reliable way of ensuring success.

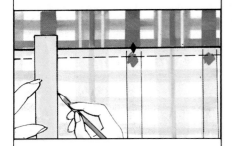

Lay the front pattern piece on the fabric so that the lines are arranged in an attractive way, with the center front centered on or mid-way between a prominent stripe or square. Pin in place and then trace the lines of the fabric pattern onto the pattern piece with a soft pencil; indicate colors with colored pencils or felt tips. Place the pattern piece which will be joined to it over the top, matching notches and seamlines. Trace the lines from the first pattern piece to the second, indicating colors as before. Pin the second pattern piece to the fabric, matching the colored lines with those of the fabric.

Inserting a shirt sleeve

This method of inserting a sleeve is traditionally used on shirts, but can be used whenever the side and sleeve seams meet at the underarm. It involves putting in the sleeve before sewing the side seam so the shirt is still flat. This can make the insertion easier than the normal set-in method.

On traditional shirt fabrics (woven cottons, wool, polyester and silk), a flat fell seam is often used. On knitted and permanent press fabrics and where there is a gathered sleeve cap, stitch the seam and then finish by zigzag stitching the seam allowances together or topstitching the seam allowances to the shirt.

Inserting the sleeve

The sleeve is inserted after the collar or other neckline finish is completed. It is always easier to work on small areas without the added weight of the whole garment, so finish the cuff opening in the sleeve before putting it in. Always pin the lower part of the sleeve into the armhole before pinning the sleeve cap, especially if it is to be gathered. Baste if necessary. Once the sleeve is in and the sleeve seam is stitched, finish the sleeve with a cuff, or elastic or binding, as appropriate.

Using a flat fell seam

Flat fell seams on armholes can be made with the seam pressed either toward the sleeve or toward the shirt. The underarm seam is always pressed toward the back. On medium-weight fabrics (poplin, gabardine, lightweight flannel), cut the seam allowance wider on the edge to be folded under. Flat fell seams can be sewn with wrong sides together and felled on the right side of the fabric. This sometimes helps to keep the topstitching straight on the right side. Baste the folds if necessary to make topstitching easier.

Additional rows of stitching can be added to the seam for a more decorative effect. Topstitch close to the armhole seam on the right side before folding under the seam allowance and stitching along the fold. Make a second row of topstitching along the fold, ⅛in from the first. This additional stitching must also be included on the underarm seam, and should balance with stitching on other seams, front band, cuffs and yoke.

Flat fell method

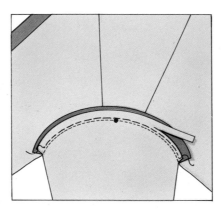

1 *Run a gathering thread around the sleeve cap to ease it into the armhole. With right sides together, pin sleeve to the armhole, matching notches and dots. Stitch and press seam toward sleeve.*

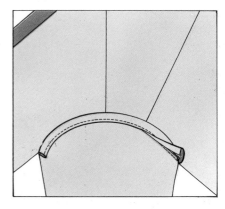

2 *Trim the sleeve seam allowance to ¼in. Fold under the shirt seam allowance, enclosing the sleeve seam allowance. Pin and stitch along the fold at an even distance (about ¼in) from the edge.*

Inserting a gathered sleeve

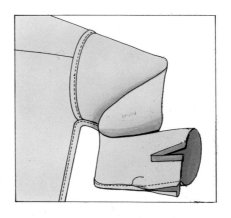

3 *Pin sleeve and side seam, matching notches, dots and armhole seam. Stitch, press toward the back, and trim the bodice back and back sleeve seam allowance. Fold under front seam allowances and stitch along the fold as before.*

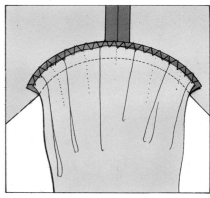

Stitch the armhole seam, distributing gathers evenly. Press the seam toward the shirt. Zigzag the seam allowances together. Alternatively, press the seam toward the shirt, clipping curves, and topstitch ¼in from seam on right side. Stitch side and sleeve seam and finish.

Kimono sleeves

Kimono sleeves, cut in one piece with the bodice, are easy to sew. The simplest shape has a shoulder line continuing straight into the top arm seam of the sleeve, and a curved underarm seam. Sometimes there is an angle at the shoulder point, which gives a close fit to the sleeve. The underarm curve may begin as low as the waist, curving into a wide or narrow sleeve (batwing/dolman/Magyar sleeves). As these types of sleeve often have a loose fit under the armhole they are most suited to fine fabrics and soft knits.

Strengthening the sleeve seam

When the arm is raised, considerable stress is put on the underarm seam, which needs strengthening. On close-fitting sleeves, a gusset may be added to relieve the strain.

If twill tape is used for strengthening, tape the most curved part of the seam; 3-4in is normally enough. When attaching the tape or sewing in a gusset, take care not to catch unwanted layers of fabric in the stitching.

Stitching a kimono sleeve
Method 1

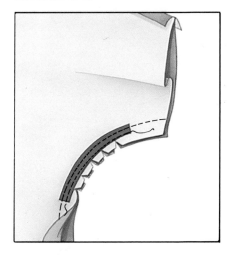

Stitch shoulder seams and press open. Pin narrow twill tape to the curve of the underarm seam on the wrong side of back garment piece. Machine stitch in place just within seam allowance. Clip curves to stitching, without clipping tape. Stitch side and underarm seam, reducing stitch length on the curve.

Method 2

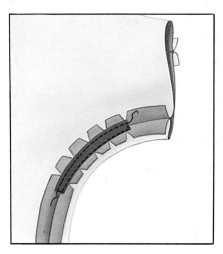

Stitch shoulder seams and press open. Stitch side and underarm seam and press open, clipping curves. On wrong side, center narrow twill tape on seamline at underarm curve and baste in place. From the right side, stitch ⅛in to each side of seamline and across ends of tape. Remove basting.

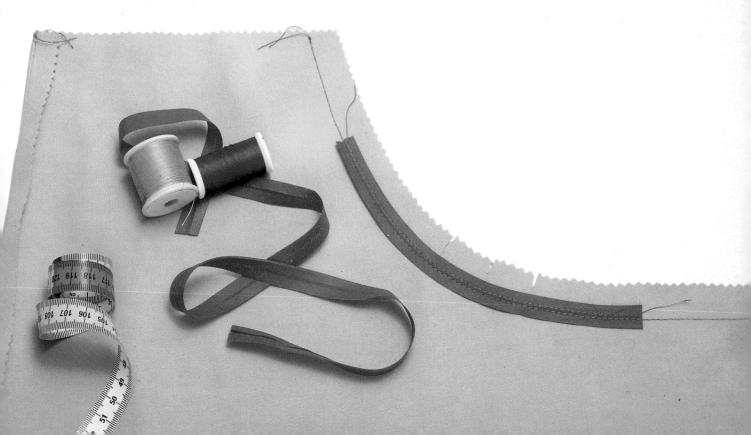

Yokes

Yokes are an interesting means of shaping, used on the bodice section of dresses, blouses and shirts, and also on trousers, shorts and skirts.

The shape of a yoke line can be straight, curved, rounded, pointed or even scalloped. The section of the garment which is attached to the yoke can be the same size, or gathered, tucked or pleated to fit the yoke. More often than not, if the yoke is the same size as the main section of the garment, shaping is incorporated into the yoke seam at bustline, waistline or hipline. Choose a yoke shape to flatter your figure.

Single and double yokes

Most yokes can be cut in single fabric. However, if you are using a fine, sheer or soft fabric, cut the yoke double. With sheer fabrics, cut the yoke facing in lining fabric and baste the sheer yoke to this piece before attaching it to the garment. This strengthens the yoke and prevents the seams from showing on the right side.

The yoke can also be cut double to finish an outer edge such as the neck edge and front opening of a dress or blouse, or the waistline edge of a skirt. A double yoke can also be treated as a single thickness and finished with a collar or waistband.

Decorative yokes

The yoke can be cut on the bias, or in the opposite direction to that of the rest of the garment. This is very effective if using striped or plaid fabric. Other ways of emphasizing the yoke include inserting cording, lace or other types of trimming into the yoke seam. If the yoke is applied to the right side of the main garment section, the edge of the yoke can be bound before being stitched in place. Another alternative is to topstitch above the yoke seamline in a matching or contrasting thread.

Attaching the yoke

There are two main methods of attaching the yoke to the garment. The first is to use a plain seam, which is suitable for single and double yokes, and the second is to turn under the yoke seam allowances and apply the yoke flat to the right side of the main garment section. This second method is ideal for a pointed yoke where it can be difficult to obtain a perfect point. The first method varies slightly with a double yoke, depending on whether the yoke is finished with another garment piece or used to finish the outer edges. In both cases the lower edge of the yoke facing is slipstitched in place.

Attaching a curved double yoke to a gathered skirt

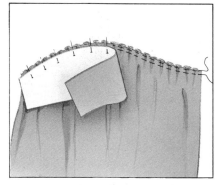

1 *Work two rows of gathering stitches along the top edge of skirt sections. With right sides together, raw edges even and center points matching, pin yokes to skirt pieces pulling up gathering threads to fit the yoke. Distribute gathers evenly and baste.*

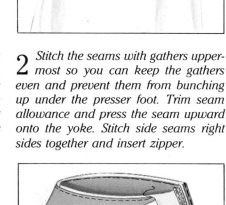

2 *Stitch the seams with gathers uppermost so you can keep the gathers even and prevent them from bunching up under the presser foot. Trim seam allowance and press the seam upward onto the yoke. Stitch side seams right sides together and insert zipper.*

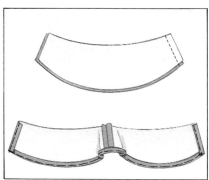

3 *With right sides together, pin, baste and stitch side seams of yoke facing, leaving the left side seam open if a zipper has been inserted in the garment. Press seam open. Turn seam allowance to wrong side along lower and side edges of facing and baste. Press flat.*

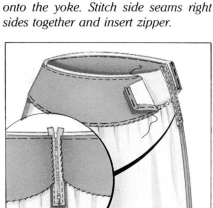

4 *With wrong sides together, raw edges even and seams and center points matching, pin yoke facing to yoke. Baste along upper and lower edges. Slipstitch yoke facing to yoke seamline, enclosing raw edges, and press. Slipstitch side edges to zipper tape. Attach waistband.*

Attaching straight double yoke to finish waist edge of pleated skirt

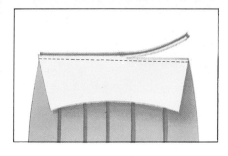  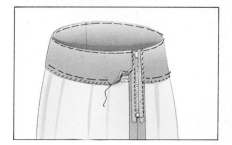

1 *Fold and baste pleats in place. With right sides together and raw edges even, pin, baste and stitch the yokes to pleated sections of the skirt. Trim seams and press upward onto yokes. Stitch side seams with right sides together and insert zipper.*

2 *Stitch right side seam of yoke facing as before. Press seam open. Turn under seam allowance at lower edge of facing, baste and press. With right sides together and top edges matching, pin and baste yoke facing to yoke. Stitch and trim seam. Clip seam allowance if seam is curved.*

3 *Press yoke facing up onto seam allowances and understitch. Turn yoke facing down to inside of garment and baste along stitched edge. Press. For a topstitched finish to the edge, omit understitching. On the inside, slipstitch lower and side edge of facing in place as before. Press.*

Attaching a single yoke to a gathered bodice

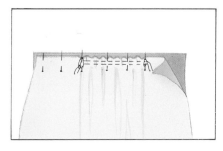 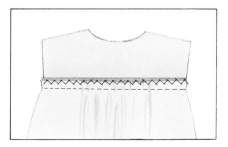

1 *Work two rows of gathering stitches along the edge to be gathered. With right sides together, raw edges even and center points matching, pin yoke to gathered section; pulling up the gathers to fit the yoke. Distribute gathers evenly and baste in place.*

2 *Stitch seam with gathers on top. Trim seam allowances to ⅜in and finish together. Press seam upward. This type of seam is often topstitched to keep the seam allowances flat.*

Attaching a single pointed yoke to a bodice

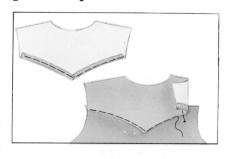 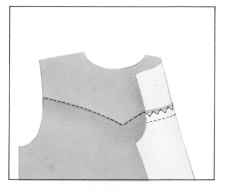

1 *Turn seam allowance to wrong side along the pointed edge of yoke and baste. Press flat. With right side of yoke and bodice facing up, lay yoke on top of bodice, matching raw edges and center points, so folded edge aligns with bodice seamline. Pin and baste.*

2 *From the right side topstitch the yoke in place, stitching close to the folded edge. Press. On the inside trim the seam allowance and finish edges together. A second row of topstitching may be worked above the first row if desired for a decorative finish.*

Attaching a simple collar

Whatever the shape of your collar, the method of attaching is the same. Interfacing is included to hold the shape of the collar and should be a weight that stiffens the fabric without making it too rigid or uncomfortable to wear. Always attach sew-in interfacing to the upper collar; iron-on to the collar facing.

The collar can be attached by machine stitching the collar facing to the neckline (as shown), or by stitching the upper collar to the neckline. This alternative method produces a neat finish on the inside edge, which is useful on open necks where the inside is visible. In this case trim and press under the seam allowance on the neck edge of the collar facing in step 1, before joining collar pieces. Mark the seamline at collar neck edge with a line of long machine stitches.

A good collar fits the neckline of the garment perfectly, which means taking special care when matching notches and stitching. If the neckline of the garment is altered—lowered or raised—a new collar will be needed. Zippers are put in before the collar is attached, buttonholes are made afterward.

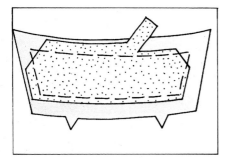

1 *Place sew-in interfacing on wrong side of one collar piece and trim outer corners ¼in inside seamline. Baste ⅛in outside seamline and trim close to stitching. Trim seam allowances from iron-on interfacing before applying. Mark seamline on the neck edge of collar, press to wrong side and trim.*

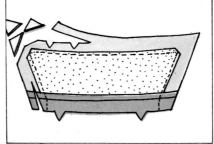

2 *With right sides together, pin collar pieces together around outer edges. Baste and stitch, shortening stitch length 1in from each corner to strengthen and making one or two stitches across point. Trim corners and grade seam allowances, trimming collar facing more than upper collar. Notch curves.*

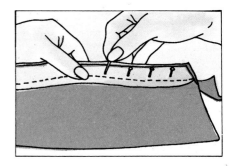

3 *Turn collar right side out, easing out the corners with a pin. Press with the seam exactly on the edge or slightly toward the collar facing. Staystitch garment neck edge ⅛in within seamline. Pin right side of collar facing to right side of garment, matching center fronts, backs and dots, as appropriate.*

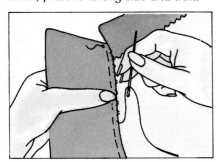

4 *Clip neck to staystitching if it helps the collar to lie flat, and baste and stitch. Clip curves and grade seam allowances, trimming more from the collar facing than from the garment. Press seam toward collar. Pin collar neck edge over stitching and slipstitch, or baste, then edgestitch it by machine. Press. Topstitch around outer edges of collar, if desired, to finish.*

Tie collars

It is very easy to add a tie collar to a pattern with a plain, front-opening neckline. Choose a fairly soft material that is not too thick or springy, so that it will tie neatly. Poplin, batiste, wool challis, single knits and crêpe are all ideal. A plaid or striped fabric looks effective when cut on the bias to contrast with a garment cut on the straight grain.

The method for attaching a tie collar is the same whether you want a neat tailored bow continuing from a narrow neckband, or a softer scarf style. The scarf style, which is cut wider, usually folds over around the neck, and is either tied in a bow, or, cut slightly shorter, worn cravat style.

Calculating the size
For a tie collar with a finished width of $\frac{3}{4}$ in or more, the neckline part of the collar should be stitched to the neckline to within about $\frac{5}{8}$ in of the center front to allow space for tying the bow. Mark these points on the pattern or garment.

To calculate the length of the tie collar, measure around the neckline between markings (or from center front to center front), then add on enough for two tie ends. Tie a tape measure around your neck to get an idea of the length required. A total length of 60in provides ties long enough for a medium-sized bow. The tie collar is made double, so allow twice the finished width, plus seam allowances.

Cutting out
The tie collar may be cut on the straight grain, or on the bias, according to the desired effect, but the wider scarf collar will drape and tie more easily when cut on the bias. This does, however, require a fair amount of fabric, as the pieces need to be cut diagonally across the length. Where joinings are needed, try to place them inconspicuously at the center back and/or concealed in the tie. The ends may be cut diagonally or squared off.

Preparing the collar
Join pieces on the straight grain to make the length required for the collar and press seams open. Mark points on each side of the center of the tie to correspond with measurement around neckline and mark center back with a line of basting for accurate positioning.

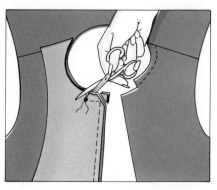

1 *Attach facings to front edges of garment, stitching only as far as center front lines or your markings. Clip into seam allowance at end of stitching, trim corners and seams, and turn facing to inside. Baste in place at neck edge.*

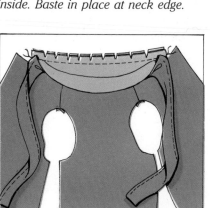

3 *Turn tie ends right side out through opening. Press seams to edge and baste. With right sides together and center back of neckline to center back of collar, stitch one open edge of collar to neck edge between markings. Fasten off threads and clip seam allowance.*

 To give a crisper finish to the neckband section of a tie collar, add a strip of interfacing between the markings. Avoid stiffening the whole length or the bow may be difficult to tie.

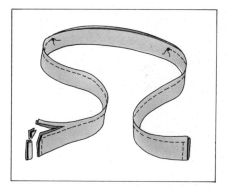

2 *With right sides together, fold tie collar in half lengthwise. Stitch across ends and along sides as far as markings, leaving center section open. Trim seams where stitched and cut away excess fabric at corners.*

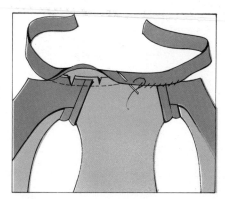

4 *Bring loose edge of collar over to inside of garment, fold under raw edge and slipstitch to neck edge along previous line of stitching. Remove basting and re-press collar and ties.*

Stand collars

The stand collar is attached to a high round neckline. The inner edge of the stand collar is much straighter than the neck edge of the garment so that it stands up against the neck when worn.

The stand collar can be made in various widths; it is important to find a width which you can wear comfortably. People with short necks often find that they have to alter the width of the collar to bring it into proportion with the length of their necks, and others may find that they cannot wear a stand collar at all. Before cutting out the collar in the garment fabric, check the width and fit of the collar. To do this it may be necessary to make up the collar in unbleached muslin or a scrap of garment fabric and try it around your neck.

If the collar is too high, alter it by trimming the required amount from the outer edge of the collar, following the original shape. Do not try to alter the neck edge.

Shirt collar with stand
The stand collar can be made into a traditional shirt collar simply by adding another collar section to the outer edge of the stand collar before it is completed.

If you have altered the width of the stand you must also alter the width of the additional collar piece by trimming the same amount from the inner edge.

Interfacing
Stand collars and shirt collars should always be interfaced to give them body and shaping. The interfacing is cut from the same pattern piece as the collar and applied to the section which is attached to the neck edge first and faces outward when the finished collar stands up around the neck.

When making a shirt collar, use either the regular weight interfacing, or a firm interfacing made specifically to stiffen shirt collars, which is available at most fabric stores. Interface the upper side of the shirt collar to prevent the seam allowance from showing on the right side. If using very firm interfacing, cut off the corners just inside the stitching line before stitching the collar pieces together so you can push out the corners to a good point. Always use sew-in rather then iron-on interfacing when stiffening the outer collar piece.

Decorative finishes
The stand collar can be trimmed with cording, a fabric ruffle or lace set into the seam around the outer edge of the collar. Alternatively the stand (and shirt collar, if appropriate) can be topstitched in a matching or contrasting thread. If the center front edges meet, they can be fastened with fabric ties, cord or ribbon stitched into the seam at the front edge of the collar. If they overlap, a decorative tie can be stitched to the center back of the stand.

Attaching the collar
There are two methods of attaching a stand collar. Which one you use depends on whether or not the garment has a front neck facing. When assembling the garment, attach the collar as soon as possible after stitching the shoulder seams to prevent the neckline from becoming stretched. It is also easier to attach the collar before stitching the side seams.

Making a stand collar

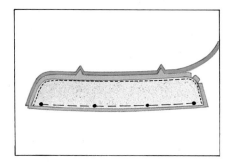

1 Baste interfacing to wrong side of one collar piece. With right sides together and notches matching, pin, baste and stitch collar pieces together around outer edge. Trim interfacing close to stitching, grade seam allowances and clip corners.

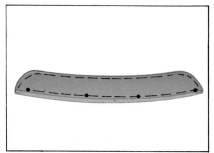

2 Turn the collar right side out. Bring the seamline to the edge of the collar by rolling the seam between the thumb and forefinger. Baste around stitched edge only and press flat.

Stand collar without front neck facing

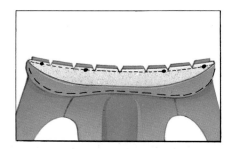

With right sides together, center backs and center fronts matching and circles at shoulders, pin, baste and stitch interfaced edges of collar to neck edge. Trim interfacing close to stitching, grade seam allowances and clip curved edges. Press seam toward collar.

Stand collar with front neck facing

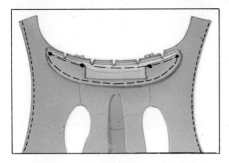

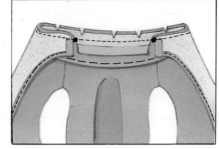

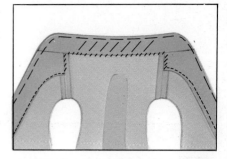

1 *Make collar and clip inner collar neck seam allowance to circles at shoulder points. With right sides together, center backs and center fronts matching, and circles at shoulders, pin and baste both collar pieces to neck edge from front edges to shoulder seams. Baste through interfaced collar piece only between circles at shoulder seams.*

2 *Fold the front neck facings back over collar with right sides together, along the fold line. Baste to neck edge through collar, turning facing seam allowance to wrong side at shoulder seams. Stitch from front edge to shoulder, then across back neck, keeping inner collar edge free, to opposite front edge.*

3 *Trim interfacing and grade and clip seam allowances. Cut across front corners. Turn facing to inside and baste along front edges. Press. Clip neck seam allowance to stitching line at shoulders and press back neck seam allowance to collar. Turn under seam allowance on inner collar and baste to neck edge. Slipstitch collar and facings.*

Finishing by hand

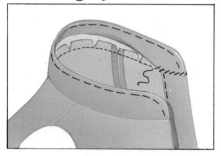

Turn ⅝in seam allowance to wrong side on free edge of inner collar piece and slipstitch to garment along the previous stitching line. Topstitch collar ⅛in in from outer edges if desired.

Finishing by machine

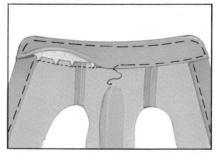

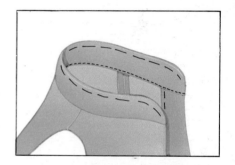

1 *Turn ½in of the ⅝in seam allowance to wrong side along free edge of inner collar piece and pin and baste to neck edge, overlapping stitching line by ⅛in.*

2 *Machine stitch along the seamline from the right side, securing the inner edge of the collar on the inside. Press. Topstitch collar ¼in in from outer edges if desired.*

Making a shirt collar

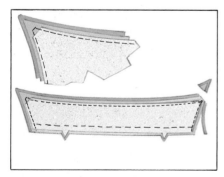

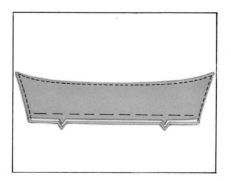

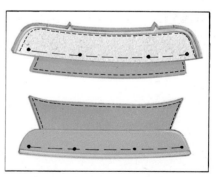

1 *Baste interfacing to wrong side of one shirt collar piece, trimming corners just inside stitching line. With right sides together, pin, baste and stitch collar pieces together around outer edges. Trim interfacing close to stitching and grade seam allowances. Cut across corners.*

2 *Turn collar right side out and bring the seam to the edge of the collar by rolling between the thumb and forefinger. Baste around outer edges and press flat. Topstitch collar ½in in from outer edges if desired.*

3 *With right sides together and the notches matching, pin and baste the collar bands to each side of collar. Stitch around outer edge of collar band as shown. Trim interfacing close to stitching and grade seam allowances. Clip curves. Turn bands right side out and press. Attach as for stand collar.*

Collars with lapels

A collar with lapels is usually worn open, and is identifiable by the distinctive V-shaped notch formed between the collar and the lapel, which is cut in one with the front. The angle of the notch may vary from a very sharp-pointed V-shape to more than a right angle. The notch may be placed high or low, according to the design, and may also have one edge longer than the other. Whatever the style, it is important to check that the length of the notches is exactly the same as at both ends of the collar, before stitching the collar in place.

Insertion method
This is the simplest way to make a collar with lapels and is most suitable for blouses and lightweight fabrics. In this method the collar is made first, and is then stitched in place by inserting the neck edge between the garment and facing. When stitching is complete, the neck seam allowances are pressed toward the bodice. This may cause too much bulk on heavier fabrics; here the flat-stitched method is more suitable.

Flat-stitched method
This method is particularly suitable for medium and heavyweight fabrics and more tailored designs. The under collar is first stitched to the neck edge of the garment, and the top collar is stitched to the neck edge of the facing. This enables the neck seams to be pressed open, so that half the neck seam allowances lie toward the collar and half toward the bodice. The collars and lapels are then stitched together around the outer edge.

Finishing flat-stitched collars
Collars applied by the flat-stitched method are joined together only at the outer edges. To prevent the two layers of the collar from slipping against each other, lightly attach the inner neck edges of the collar together. This additional strengthening is done by lifting the back neck facing and stitching the back neck seam allowances together with a loose running stitch between the shoulder seams. Leave the stitches fairly loose to allow the collar a little movement to form a natural roll line.

Pressing
To achieve a crisp edge, first press seams open where possible. Around collar, notch and lapels, press the seam just slightly to the underside of the collar to give a neat finish to the top collar and lapels. At the lower end of the lapels gradually change the roll of the seam, first to the very edge, then over slightly to the underside of the front for the remainder of the front edge.

Flat-stitched method

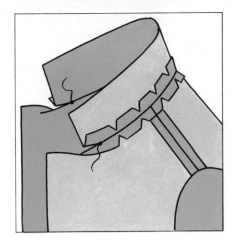

1 With right sides together, stitch neck edge of under collar to neck edge of garment between inner lapel markings. In same way stitch top collar to neck facing. Trim and clip seam allowances and press seams open.

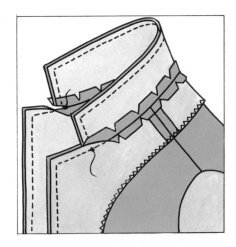

2 With right sides facing and edges even, stitch collar together around outer edge between inner lapel markings. Turn the neck seam allowance upward at top of lapels and stitch facing to front from inner lapel marking to lower edge of front. Trim seam allowances. Turn the collar right side out and press.

Insertion method

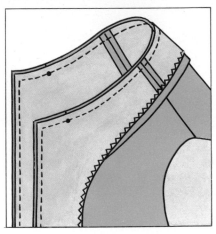

1 Make and press collar. With right side of garment and top side of collar uppermost, pin collar around neck edge with ends of collar matching inner lapel markings. Baste in place.

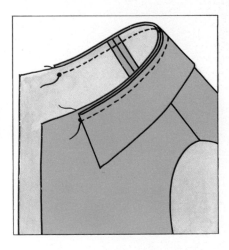

2 Make neck facing. With right sides together and edges even, stitch facing around front and neck edges so collar is sandwiched between the facing and garment. Trim seam allowance and corners. Clip seam allowance around neck. Turn right side out and press.

Making a shawl collar

Shawl collars may be cut with a separate under collar, which is stitched to the front, or they can be cut with the front pattern extended to include the under collar, which is joined at the center back neckline. It should roll over smoothly to form a stand around the neck. A facing is added to the fronts of the garment and extends to become the top collar.

Styles
A shawl collar may follow a slim, narrow shape, or have a generous curve, according to the design. It can have a long roll line which extends to the waist and wraps, or it may fasten in a fairly high V-shaped neckline. The outer edge of the collar can be topstitched, edged with braid or a ruffle, or scalloped.

Fabrics
Any fairly soft fabric that will roll well is suitable for this type of collar. Avoid very thick or stiff fabric which may not set into an attractive rolled line.

Interfacing
Use a suitable interfacing to support the fabric without stiffening it. Use either a sew-in or iron-on type according to the garment fabric. If possible test first for the best effect.

Notched shawl collars
A mock lapel can be made from a basic shawl collar pattern by stitching and cutting out a V-shaped notch from the outer edge of the collar before turning it right side out. To do this, decide upon the desired notch size and position and mark it evenly on the collar pattern. Transfer the markings from the pattern to both halves of collar and facing pieces.

Making a shawl collar

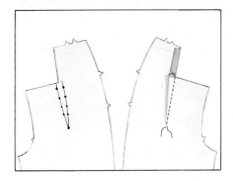

1 If there is a dart in the side neckline of the front, stitch this first and press toward center front. Clip diagonally into corner to release back neck edge of under collar.

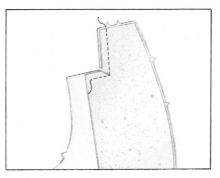

2 Apply interfacing to the attached under collar on fronts. Staystitch along back neck edge and around corner onto shoulder edge. Clip corner diagonally to stitching.

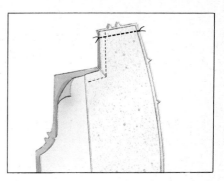

3 With right sides together and notches matching, stitch fronts together along center back neck edges. Trim seam allowances and press seam open.

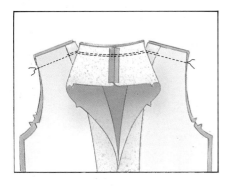

4 With right sides together, place front on back and baste shoulder seams. Baste under collar edge to back neckline. Beginning at outer edge, stitch one shoulder seam, leave needle in fabric at corner, rearrange fabric, pivot work, and stitch across back neckline. Pivot again and stitch shoulder seam.

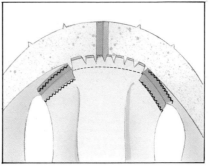

5 Clip seam allowances across back neck seam, taking care not to cut the stitching. Press both seam allowances up toward collar. Press shoulder seams open and finish edges with medium-width zigzag stitching.

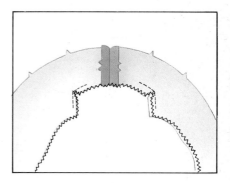

6 With right sides together and the notches matching, join center back seam of front facing/top collar pieces. Press seam open. Staystitch the inner corners of the neckline and clip to the stitching at the corners. Finish entire inner edge of facing with zigzag stitching.

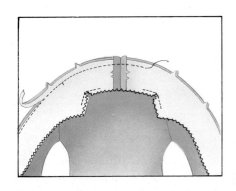

7 With right sides together, place the facing/top collar on garment with seams and notches matching. Stitch together around outer edge. Grade seam allowances to reduce bulk. Clip seam on deep curves.

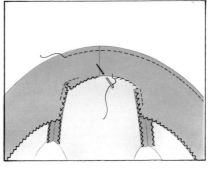

8 Turn facing over to inside and bring seam to edge. Baste edge and press. Finish back neck by turning the seam allowance under and slipstitching, or by stab stitching through the seam from the underside on thicker fabrics. Herringbone stitch remaining edges of facing to shoulder seams.

Notched shawl collar

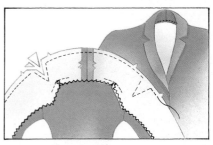

Mark notch shape on pattern at suitable position and transfer to both halves of front and facing pieces. Stitch around outer edge as in step 7 but following the marked notch shapes. Cut into the notches and trim the corners before turning right side out and finishing as described in step 8.

Cuff openings

This type of opening is made at the cuff edge of the sleeve before the underarm seam is stitched, and gives a bound finish which is hidden when the cuff is closed. It is widely used on shirts, blouses, dresses and sometimes on lightweight outer garments. It is suitable only for light and medium weight fabrics, as the seam allowances on thick fabrics are too bulky and cause gaping when the cuff is closed.

The position of the opening is usually shown by a line on the back edge of the sleeve pattern piece. However, if you wish to incorporate this type of opening on a sleeve which does not have the opening marked, you can mark the position yourself. Draw a vertical line $2\frac{3}{4}$-$3\frac{1}{2}$in long (child/adult sizes) from the lower edge at the center of the back half of the sleeve pattern.

Cutting the binding

The binding is usually made from a bias strip 1in wide and twice the length of the opening. On slightly thicker fabrics the binding can be cut $1\frac{1}{4}$in wide to permit the seam allowances to lie flatter inside the binding.

Preparing the opening

Always reinforce the opening with staystitching before attaching the bias strip. Stitch along both sides of the slash line, starting $\frac{1}{4}$in from the line at the lower edge, tapering to a point at the top of the marking and then stitching back to the lower edge to finish $\frac{1}{4}$in from the slash line.

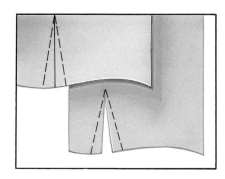

1 *Mark the center slash line on the wrong side of the sleeve using basting stitches or tailor's chalk. Reinforce the opening with staystitching. Cut along the slash line to the point of the stitching, taking care not to cut through the stitches themselves.*

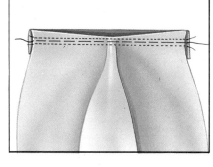

2 *Open out the slash in the sleeve until it is straight. Pin and baste the bias strip to the opening with right sides together and the line of staystitching ¼in from the raw edge of the strip. Stitch the strip to the opening along the line of staystitching.*

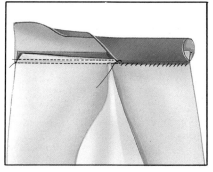

3 *Press the seam allowances toward the strip. Turn ¼in to the wrong side along the free edge of the strip, fold to the inside of the sleeve and slipstitch the folded edge to the sleeve along the stitching line. Press flat.*

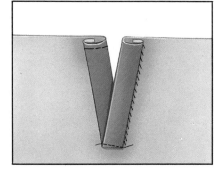

4 *Turn the front section of the strip completely to the wrong side and baste to the sleeve at the lower edge. Leave the back section of the strip flat. Stitch across folded edge of binding at top of opening to hold in place.*

Straight lapped cuff

The straight lapped cuff is a very popular way of finishing the lower edge of a sleeve and is used on a wide variety of clothing. It can be cut on the straight grain of the fabric or on the bias, which adds a decorative effect if you are using striped or plaid fabric.

The cuff is used with a continuous strip opening in the sleeve and is put on after the opening and underarm seam have been completed. The sleeve can be gathered or tucked to fit the cuff. A small section of this cuff extends beyond the back sleeve edge so that when the cuff is fastened, the front of the cuff overlaps it.

The front edge of the cuff can be shaped with a point or rounded. These different finishes can often be worked more easily if the cuff is cut in two sections and seamed along the lower edge. In this case, join the two sections along the lower edge before attaching the cuff to the sleeve.

Interfacing

Cuffs should always be interfaced to give them body. Choose a suitable interfacing and — if it is sew-in — apply it to the part of the cuff that will lie on the outside; if it is iron-on, to the inner part. Assemble and attach the cuff to the sleeve. For a straight cuff, cut the interfacing half the width of the cuff or to the fold line. For a shaped cuff, use the cuff pattern piece and apply to one section of each cuff.

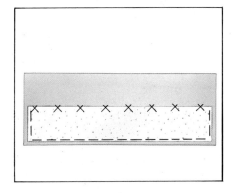

1 Cut the interfacing to size and baste to the wrong side of half the cuff as shown. Catch in place along the fold line, using herringbone stitch.

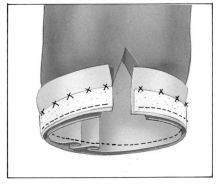

2 Pin and baste interfaced edge of cuff to lower edge of sleeve. Stitch from edge of back opening to edge of front opening. Grade the seam allowances, trimming interfacing close to stitching. Press seam toward cuff.

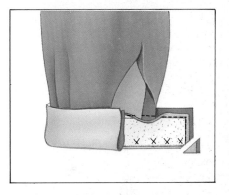

3 With right sides together, fold cuff along fold line. Baste and stitch across the end and along the small seam extending beyond the sleeve at the back edge of cuff. Clip corners.

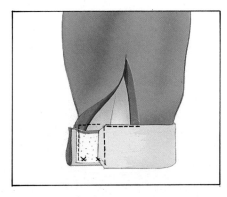

4 Baste and stitch the straight seam at the front edge of the cuff. Grade seam allowances, trimming the interfacing close to the stitching, and trim corners as before.

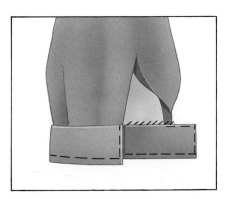

5 Turn cuff right side out and baste around outer edge. Press. On inside of sleeve, turn in seam allowance on free edge of cuff and slipstitch folded edge to stitching line. Press.

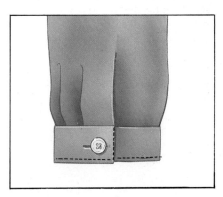

6 On the right side, topstitch ¼in in from outer edges of cuff. (This topstitching is optional.) Make the fastening as desired, finishing with a snap (and optional decorative button) or a button and buttonhole.

French cuff

French cuffs are no more complicated to make than straight band cuffs and they add a discreet touch of stylish detail to a woman's shirt. They are also used on men's dress shirts, where they are more commonly called double shirt cuffs.

French cuffs fold back on themselves when worn to form a double cuff. One-piece cuffs are cut four times the depth of the folded cuff depth, plus two seam allowances. For an average fit, cut the length to the wrist measurement plus $2\frac{1}{2}$in plus two seam allowances. For a tighter fit, cut the length to the wrist measurement plus 2in plus two seam allowances.

Interfacing

Because French cuffs are worn folded back, the underside of the cuff (when laid out flat) becomes the right side of the folded cuff. If you wish the interfaced half of the cuff to be the finished right side of the cuff, stitch the interfaced half of the cuff to the sleeve first. If you would rather the non-interfaced half of the cuff formed the right side, stitch this to the sleeve first.

HELPING HAND

Linked buttons

Linked buttons are formed by stitching two buttons together back to back, leaving a $\frac{3}{8}$-$\frac{5}{8}$in long shank of threads between them. Work buttonhole stitch along the shank to form a strong link. Use buttonhole twist for durability.

Fastenings

French cuffs may be fastened by the link method, in which a buttonhole is made in both layers at each end of the cuff. Cuff links or linked buttons are then threaded through the double buttonholes. Alternatively, the underlayer only can be fastened with a button and buttonhole and the top layer of the cuff left loose so that the corners stand out crisply.

Making the cuff

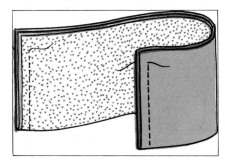

Apply interfacing lengthwise to half the cuff. With right sides facing fold cuff in half along edge of interfacing. Stitch across ends, finishing stitching ⅝in from raw edges. Trim seams, clip corners, turn right side out and press seams to edge of cuff.

Applying the cuff

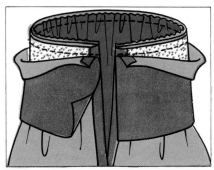

With right side of cuff to wrong side of sleeve, and ends of cuff level with edges of sleeve opening, stitch one edge of cuff to sleeve. Trim seam and press seam allowance into cuff.

Finishing a linked cuff

Tuck in seam allowance along remaining loose edge of cuff and machine stitch to right side of sleeve along previous stitching line. Fold back cuff and press. Make corresponding buttonholes on the center of both layers of the cuff at each end.

Finishing a buttoned cuff

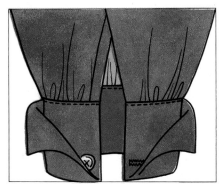

Complete cuff as for linked cuff by folding under seam allowance on loose edge of cuff and machine stitching to right side of sleeve, along the previous stitching line. Fold back the cuff and press. At front end of cuff make a buttonhole the diameter of the button above the fold line on the underlayer of cuff only. Sew button to the underlayer at the back end of cuff to correspond.

Patch pockets

Patch pockets are made from a separate piece of fabric which is topstitched to the right side of a garment. They can be almost any shape —square, oblong, round, triangular or heart-shaped. They can be strictly functional, or combine usefulness with a decorative effect by using contrasting fabric, fabric cut on the bias, or by adding embroidery or inserting a decorative trim around the edge.

Pockets with attached facing

The simplest patch pockets have an attached facing across the top. First finish top edge, then fold facing over to right side along fold line. Stitch facing to pocket at sides. Trim top corners, turn right side out and press.

Pockets with a shaped top edge

These have the top edge finished with a separate facing. First finish lower edge of facing, then with right sides together, stitch facing to pocket at side and top edges. Trim seams and corners, turn right side out and press.

Lined pockets

Self-lined pockets are made from double thickness fabric and are not suitable for thick fabrics. This method is good for rounded pockets, as the stitching line helps to achieve a smooth curve. It is less suitable for square pockets, where it can be difficult to get crisp corners, especially on thicker fabrics. Line square pockets and pockets made in thicker fabrics with lining fabric.

Stitching

On a plain pocket the facing can be left loose inside the pocket. Alternatively, the lower edge of the facing can be topstitched to the pocket for a decorative effect. If the edge of the facing is shaped, topstitch following the shaped line of the facing.

Strengthen top corners of a pocket by either machine stitching a triangle, or working a double row of topstitching on sporty styles.

Square pocket with attached facing

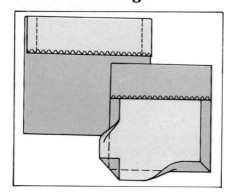

Finish attached facing as decribed above and then press seam allowance to wrong side along side and lower edges to establish corner point. Unfold corners and press corner to wrong side, in line with corner point. Press sides and lower edge so they meet at the corner in a neat miter.

Rounded pocket with shaped top edge

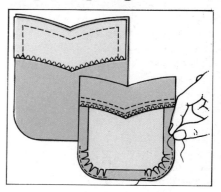

Finish shaped top edge as described above and then stitch a long machine stitch around corners just outside the stitching line. Press seam allowance to wrong side on straight edges. Pull up thread to ease rounded corners so that stitching rolls to wrong side. Notch seam allowance on curve and press.

Lined pockets

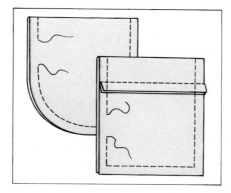

On a self-lined pocket, fold pocket in half, right sides together. Stitch around side and lower edge, leaving an opening at an inconspicuous part of a straight edge. Turn right side out. Press seam, continuing with a good line across opening. The pocket topstitching will close the opening. Attach a separate lining to edge of attached facing, right sides together. Complete in same way.

Attaching the pocket

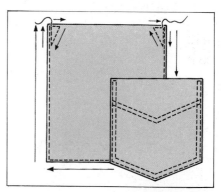

Stitch strengthening triangle, starting at top right corner, stitching down side for ½in and turning to form triangle. Continue around pocket and work opposite corner in reverse. Alternatively, stitch outer row of topstitching around pocket from top right corner. At top left corner, turn, stitch across top for three or four stitches and stitch inner row with side of presser foot against first row as a guide.

Pockets in a seam

Pockets in a seam are more practical than other types of pocket, as most pockets distort in use and often spoil the look of the garment. A pocket in a seam can be completely hidden in a side or front panel seam, or topstitched on the right side of the garment as a fashion detail. The pocket can be cut in one with the main garment pieces, or as separate pieces which are then stitched to the main pieces at the appropriate position.

Separate pocket pieces
Separate pocket pieces can be stitched directly to the front and back at side or front panel seams, or to an extension on the main garment pieces. Extensions have the advantage of hiding the pocket fabric from view when the pockets gape in use. This is particularly useful with heavyweight fabrics, when the front pocket pieces can be cut from matching lightweight fabric or lining fabric to reduce bulk. If the extension is not cut in one with the main garment piece, stitch a strip of the main fabric to the seam to form an extension before adding the pocket piece.

Reinforcing the pocket
The pocket opening can be reinforced with seam binding or iron-on interfacing to prevent the pocket from gaping. This is particularly useful on bias or stretchy seams. Cut the binding 2in longer than the opening and stitch to the wrong side of the front garment piece, just within the seam allowance. Apply interfacing in a similar way. Soft iron-on interfacing can also be applied to the back pocket pieces to help keep the pocket flat in use.

Stitching the pocket
The corners of the pocket take most of the strain, so this angle must be cleanly and strongly stitched. Stitch garment seams together along the seamline using shorter stitches near the corners for extra strength. Leave the needle in the fabric at the corners, raise the presser foot and pivot the fabric before resuming stitching. Another method of strengthening pocket corners is to reverse stitch each side of the pivot.

Adding a pocket
If you are adding pockets to an existing pattern, place your hands at your hips to find a comfortable position for the pocket and measure from your waist to the top of your hand. Mark this measurement on the side or front panel seam on the pattern, and the base of the opening some 6in below. Draw the outline of the pocket from the pocket opening on the pattern, using a flexible curve and making sure that the pocket is big enough to take your hand. Trace the pocket shape from the pattern and add seam allowances all around. Add seam allowances to top and bottom of pocket opening on the main garment pattern piece and add an extension the width of the seam allowance between these two points.

Attaching the pockets

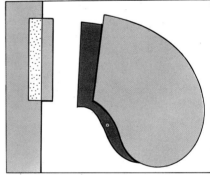

1 *To prepare separate pocket pieces, cut out main garment pieces with extension at pocket position and pocket shapes, cutting the front pocket piece in lining fabric if this reduces bulk. Apply a strip of interfacing along the pocket opening, within the seam allowance.*

 Mark the stitching lines on the wrong side of both attached and separate pockets before moving the pattern piece. This will give you a good guide for stitching an even line.

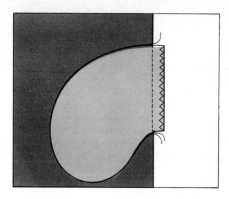 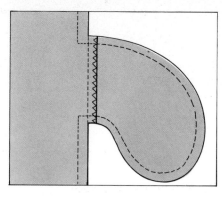 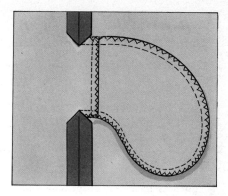

2 *With right sides together, stitch pocket pieces to extensions, with the bag of the pocket facing downward. Press seams as stitched, trim seam allowances and finish edges together with zigzag stitch. Press seam allowances toward pocket.*

3 *To join pocket pieces on separate and attached pockets, stitch side seam and pocket in one continuous seam, with front and back pieces right sides together. Reduce stitch length at corners of pocket opening to give added strength. Press seams as stitched.*

4 *Clip the seam allowance on the back of the garment at top and bottom of the pocket. Press garment side seam open and pocket toward the front of the garment Finish raw edges of pocket together with zigzag stitch and press flat.*

Topstitched finish

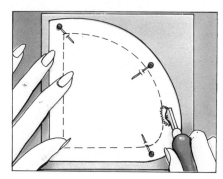

1 *When topstitching the pocket to the front of the garment, make a template of the finished pocket shape to help achieve a good stitching line. Transfer stitching lines of pocket to heavy paper using dressmaker's carbon paper and a tracing wheel and cut out along stitching lines.*

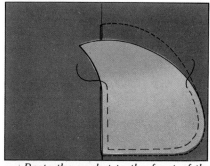

2 *Baste the pocket to the front of the main garment piece to hold it in place, then pin and baste the pocket pattern to the garment, aligning the straight end of the pattern with the pocket opening. Topstitch pocket to garment from the right side, following edge of pattern. Remove pattern and basting.*

Welt pockets

Fashion interest in pocket styles varies from the concealed set-in pocket to the patch pocket. Whatever the style, a pocket must be marked, cut and stitched accurately. Pressing is very important. Do not overpress your pocket, but press each step as it is completed.

The welt pocket is a set-in pocket which is constructed from two pocket sections and a welt piece. The welt extends above the pocket to cover the opening and can be cut in self fabric or a contrasting color. If the fabric is not firmly woven, interface half of the welt to give added body. The pocket pieces are cut in self fabric if using lightweight fabric, or in lining fabric if using a heavyweight fabric.

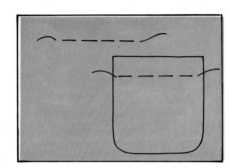

1 *Mark the position of the pocket opening on the right side of the garment with basting, as accurately as possible. Mark the pocket pieces in the same way.*

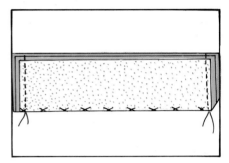

2 *Baste interfacing to one half of the pocket welt piece and catch to fold line using herringbone stitch. Fold welt in half lengthwise, right sides together. Baste and stitch across each end. Trim interfacing and seam allowances and cut diagonally across corners.*

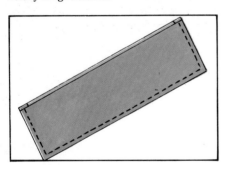

3 *Turn the welt right side out, bring seams to edge and baste around edges. Press. Topstitch the welt at this stage if desired.*

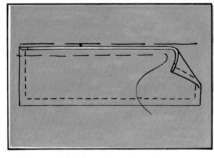

4 *Pin welt to right side of garment, with folded edge facing downward and raw edge level with the marking for the opening. Baste along seamline, ¼ in from raw edges.*

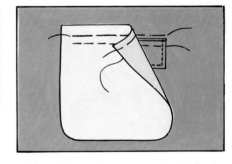

5 *Pin and baste one pocket section to the garment, right sides together, accurately matching markings for the pocket lining.*

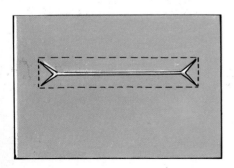

6 *Turn garment wrong side out. Stitch all around the pocket marking, taking a ¼ in seam allowance. Slash between stitching and clip into corners.*

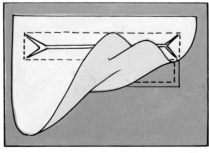

7 *Take pocket piece through opening to wrong side, bring seams to edge and baste around opening. Press welt section up over opening.*

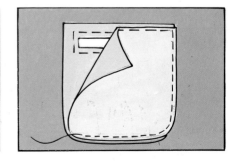

8 *On the wrong side pin and baste the second pocket section over the first, matching outer raw edges and stitching through pocket sections only.*

FASTENINGS
Belts and belt carriers

A belt can add a professional finish to your outfit as well as serving a useful purpose. Although the pattern will state the type of belt to be used, often the appearance of the garment can be altered merely by changing the belt. Different fabrics will give different effects. You can use the same fabric as used in the garment, a plain color to match one of the colors in a fabric, a contrasting color or a different texture. If you are making your own belt, choose one which is suited to the garment and your figure. Remember: the wider and more conspicuous the belt, the more attention you will draw to your waistline. Cut several belts of different widths in brown paper and try them on with the garment to find the right proportions.

Tie belts
Tie belts are very popular on dresses, coats, and other garments. They are easy to make and can be made from all kinds of fabric. If the fabric does not have a great deal of body, the belt will require interfacing. Match the weight of the interfacing to the weight of the fabric.

When cutting a tie belt, cut the fabric on the lengthwise grain to the length required by twice the desired width, plus $\frac{3}{8}$in seam allowances all around.

To determine the length of a tie belt, tie string or ribbon in a bow around your waist and cut to the required length. Use this as a guide for the length of your tie belt.

Tubing tie belts
Tubing tie belts can also be very attractive. For a firm tubing tie belt, make a length of corded tubing (see page 76), using filler cord as a stiffening. This cord can be purchased in various sizes, so choose the width most suitable for your belt. The belt can be made as a single length, or three lengths can be braided together. Remember to allow extra length if braiding three lengths together, as the braiding will take up some of the length. The ends can be left braided for a tassel effect or tied in a knot.

Belt carriers
Belt carriers are used to hold a belt neatly in position at the waistline. They can be made from narrow tubes of fabric or from thread. They are used on the waistbands of skirts and pants, and at the side seams of full length garments. Generally two to six carriers are used around the waistline. Fabric carriers vary in width from $\frac{1}{4}$–$\frac{1}{2}$in, depending on the garment and the fabric. The finished length of both fabric and thread carriers should be $\frac{1}{4}$in longer than the width of the belt, so that the belt can slip through easily. Allow an extra $\frac{5}{8}$in for turning under at top and bottom.

When cutting fabric carriers, cut a strip of fabric on the lengthwise grain, twice the finished width plus $\frac{1}{2}$in for seam allowances, and long enough to make the number of carriers required.

Belt loops differ from belt carriers in that each is attached to the garment at one point only; the ends are joined to form a ring. To make a loop, cut a strip of fabric on the lengthwise grain to twice the finished width plus $\frac{1}{2}$in for seam allowances, and long enough to make the number of loops required, allowing twice the belt width plus $\frac{1}{2}$in seam allowance for each loop.

Thread carriers are less conspicuous and are used on fine fabrics, dresses and lightweight clothing, especially evening wear. They are made of several strands of thread which are held together with buttonhole stitches.

Making a tie belt

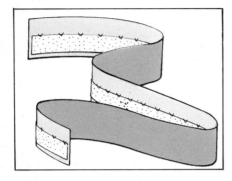 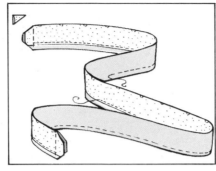 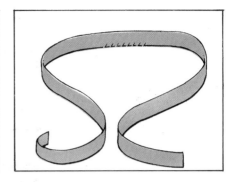

1 To interface a tie belt made in lightweight fabric, cut the interfacing to half the width of the belt. Baste to the wrong side of belt, with one edge to the center and catch to belt along center fold using herringbone stitch.

2 Fold the fabric in half lengthwise, right sides together. Pin, baste and stitch across each end and along the length to within 2in of the center, taking ⅜in seam. Press seams open with the point of the iron and trim corners.

3 Turn the belt right side out, using a blunt knitting needle to ease out corners. Turn under the seam allowances at the opening and neatly slipstitch the folded edges together. Press to achieve crisp edges.

Tubing belt

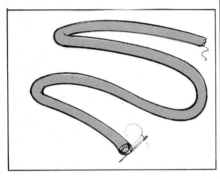

Make some corded tubing. Turn right side out and trim the cord at the center of its length, close to stitching. Slipstitch the fabric together to cover the trimmed end. Cut cord ⅜in shorter than the fabric at other end, turn in raw edges and slipstitch together as before.

Fabric belt carriers

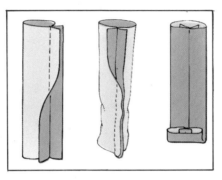 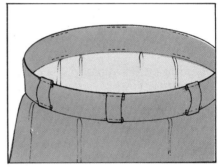

1 Fold the fabric strip lengthwise, right side inside, and stitch ¼in from the edge. Trim the seam allowance to ⅛in. Ease the seam to the center of the strip and press open with the fingers. Turn right side out, fold under ¼in at each end and press.

2 Mark the position for the finished length of carriers on the garment band. If the carriers are being attached to a finished waistband or at the side seam of a garment, either overcast or machine stitch across each end of carrier in position, on right side of band.

Belt loops

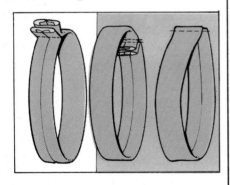 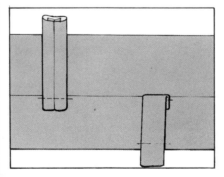 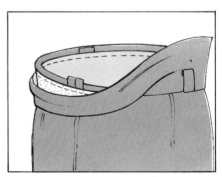

Cut a length of fabric for each loop. Complete strip as for fabric belt carriers. Place ends together with wrong sides of strip facing outward. Stitch ends together ¼in from raw edge and turn right side out. Pin loops in place and stitch across loop just above joining seam.

3 To attach carriers on an unfinished waistband, mark the position for each carrier on the band. Machine stitch one end of each carrier in position on right side at center of band. Fold carriers down and baste free end of carrier to raw edge of waistband.

4 Pin baste and stitch waistband to garment, right sides together, securing carriers in place between waistband and garment. Complete waistband in usual way by turning to inside, turning under seam allowance and slipstitching along previous stitching line.

Making a stiff belt

A belt is an important feature of a garment. Whether you make it in matching or in contrasting fabric, it must be made well, and to achieve this it is essential to use the right materials.

Choosing the stiffening
Stiffened belts have a crisper, neater look than soft tie belts. They are made with a specially treated backing called belting, which will not lose its stiffness when it is washed or dry cleaned. Belting can be purchased by the yard and is available in different widths. The width of the belting is the width the finished belt will be.

If you cannot find a commercial belting in the width you require, use stiff grosgrain ribbon. Interfacing may also be used for stiffening, but it makes a much softer belt.

Selecting a buckle
There is a vast range of buckles in different shapes, sizes and colors and others which you can cover yourself. When choosing a buckle take a piece of fabric along to help select the correct color and a suitable shape. Whether you choose a slip-on buckle without a prong, or a pronged buckle, it will need to be $\frac{1}{8}$in wider at the cross-bar than the finished width of the belt.

Cutting the fabric
Having decided on the width of the belt, buy stiffening which measures slightly less than the belt width by the waist measurement plus 10in for an overlap. Cut fabric along the lengthwise grain to the same length as the stiffening by twice the width plus $\frac{3}{8}$in seam allowance all around.

The shape at the end of the overlap can vary from a round end to a pointed end. This shape will determine where the seam will lie, and also whether the belt needs to be cut in one or two pieces. Most belts can be cut in one piece except those with both long edges shaped, which are cut in two pieces.

To make a straight belt with a shaped end you will need to shape the end of the belt before stitching the long edges together. This will enable the seam to lie in the center of the underside of the belt, rather than along one edge.

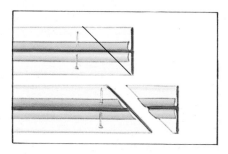

1 *To shape the end bring the two long edges of fabric together at the center with seamlines matching and pin. Draw desired shape across end with tailor's chalk. Trim end to shape.*

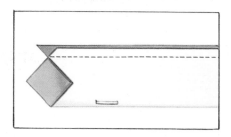

3 *With right sides together and raw edges even, fold the fabric in half lengthwise and stitch ⅜in in from the long raw edge.*

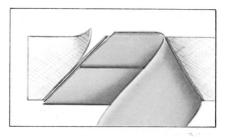

5 *Turn belt right side out by pushing the safety pin toward the open end and working the belt back over it. Arrange end stitching at the edge of the belt and seam at center of underside; press. Lay belt on stiffening ⅜in in from end and mark shape on stiffening. Trim stiffening to shape.*

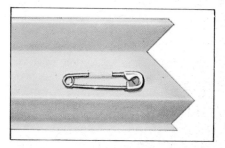

2 *Remove pins and unfold belt. Fasten a safety pin on the right side of the fabric about 1½in from the shaped end. This will be used later to turn the belt right side out.*

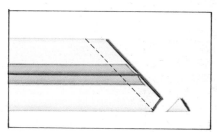

4 *Refold fabric so seam is at center and press seam allowances open. Stitch across end following shape. Trim corners; clip notches in end if curved.*

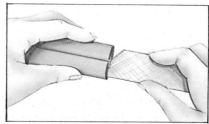

6 *Insert the shaped end of the stiffening into the belt, cupping the edges of the stiffening slightly between the thumb and forefinger. Press flat.*

Attaching a slip-on buckle

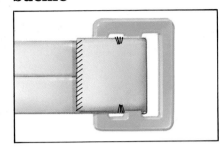

Attaching a pronged buckle

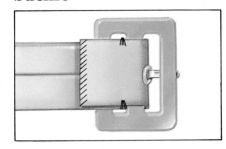

7 *At the unfinished end of the belt tuck the raw edges of the fabric to the inside of the belt, finger press and slipstitch the edges together.*

For a slip-on buckle, insert the straight end through the buckle and around the center bar. Overcast the ends firmly to the back of the belt and at each side to prevent the buckle from slipping.

For a pronged buckle, insert a metal eyelet or make a hand-worked eyelet 1in from the straight end. Insert prong through eyelet and stitch buckle in place. Try on belt, mark eyelet positions at shaped end and make to match buckle eyelet.

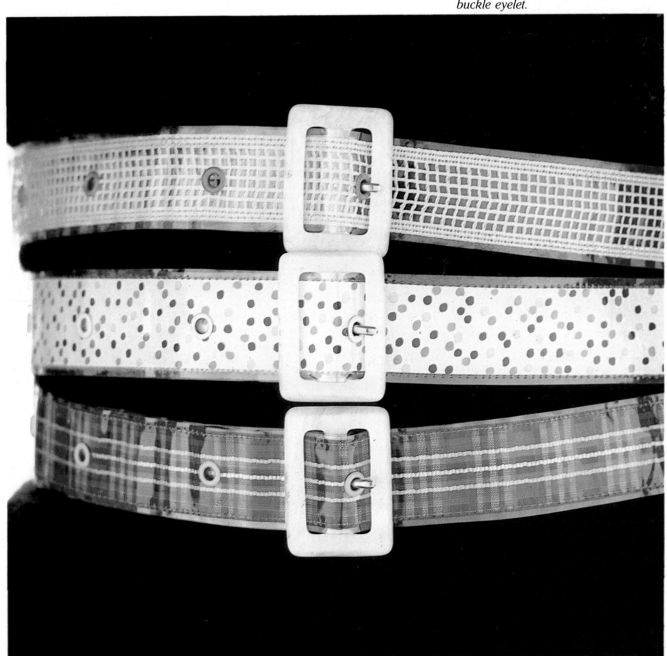

Using buttons

uttons can add a decorative touch to your clothes besides serving a purpose. Take your fabric with you when choosing from the wide selection of wood, plastic, leather, metal (beware sharp edges), hand-painted, fabric-covered, or crochet buttons available. Find a type that complements your fabric color and design. Too heavy a button will pull on the fabric. Irregular shapes are attractive but can cause wear and tear, so consider attaching them only as decoration on the fabric, with a snap underneath.

Choice of thread
For sewing on buttons choose a strong thread, suitable for the weight and type of fabric. Polyester thread is ideal for synthetics, cotton-wrapped polyester for natural fabrics, buttonhole twist for heavier ones. Secure the ends firmly with backstitches: it is frustrating to be unable to replace a lost button. Sew buttons tight enough not to flop but not so tight as to pull on the fabric. Sew through the eyes often enough to be secure (about five times with a doubled thread).

Positioning buttons
Re-measure the button spacing if you have altered the length of your garment, and try it on to check for gaping, especially at bust, waist and hips. You may need to add a hidden snap if you want to group-space your buttons, or give impressive buttons enough space between them. Pin the garment closed, matching hems and center front lines, and pin through the buttonholes to mark the position for the center of the buttons. If the buttons are to be set on the back of a dress or blouse, get a helper to check that there are no ugly gaps below your shoulders either. For horizontal buttonholes the pin should be near the edge and for vertical buttonholes the pin should be placed at the center. Buttons should be in a straight line,

normally on the center front or center back line of the garment.

Shanks
A shank should be made to the thickness of the buttonhole and is necessary to prevent the fabric from pulling under the button. A type with a ready-made shank should be sewn with the shank in line with the buttonhole. On bulky fabrics a handmade thread shank is necessary, as for all sew-through buttons. Only decorative buttons need no shank.

Making a thread shank

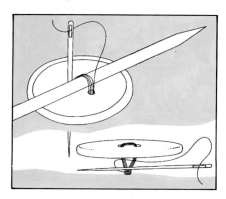

Take stitches up through fabric and button and over a matchstick, toothpick or pin to make required shank length. After stitching, remove pin and wind thread tightly around stitches under the button. Backstitch into shank to fasten off.

A strong back button

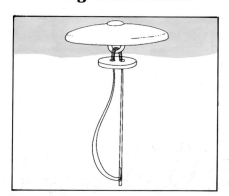

To prevent strain on heavy or loose-weave fabrics, sew directly between the top button and a small flat button at the back. Make a thread shank of the appropriate length for the top button as shown above.

Four-eye buttons

The crossover method is used only if there is a dip between the eyes, so use parallel stitches or the arrowhead shown. This is distinctive in a shiny or contrasting thread, provided the thread is not too thick.

Linked buttons

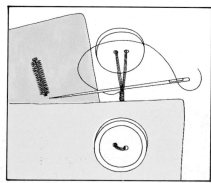

This is a useful method for bulky fabrics meeting edge to edge on a coat front or for cuffs. Form three loops over a few fingers, threading the second button onto these loops. Blanket-stitch over threads and fasten.

Covered buttons

For a really professional finish to a garment it is essential to choose suitable buttons. Despite the wide range available you may find that you cannot match a particular color or find one size you need, in which case it is better to make your own. This is done by covering purchased button molds with your chosen fabric.

Button molds
Button molds are usually plastic or metal, or a combination of both. They consist of a convex button shape, over which the fabric is stretched, and a back section which holds the fabric in place. They are available in a variety of sizes, so choose a size as close as possible to that recommended on your pattern. Button forms may vary slightly with each manufacturer, but the basic ways of covering them are the same. Button molds are shanked and they should be sewn to the fabric with the shank in line with the buttonhole.

Suitable fabrics
Most fabrics are suitable for covering button molds, apart from very thick fabrics and those that fray easily. When using fine or slightly transparent fabrics you may need to cover the button mold with two layers of fabric for a better finish. Run a gathering thread through both layers and treat as one. Light and medium-weight leathers can be used very successfully on button molds, especially those which have a serrated edge on the reverse of the front section. Stiff fabrics are easier to work with when damp. If you find it difficult to snap the back washer in position, place a spool upright over the shank with the back section below, and push, or gently hammer in place.

Buttons from rings
Ordinary curtain rings can be used to make flat, fabric-covered buttons. The fabric should be fairly closely-woven so that the ring will not shine through it. The center, flat part of the button can be

decorated with embroidery, if desired. Work the embroidery before cutting out the fabric, taking care to stay within the available space. A thread shank (see page 79) must be worked when attaching this kind of button.

Covering button molds

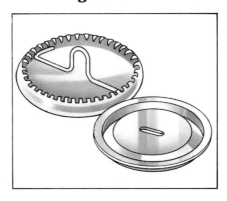

1 *Separate the two parts of the button. Cut out a circle of fabric approximately twice the width of the button front. (Some manufacturers give exact cutting size on the pack.) Knit fabrics should be cut slightly smaller since they will stretch when used.*

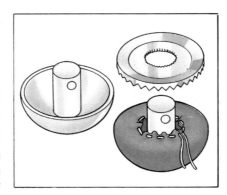

3 *When the button has a serrated edge on the back washer, work small running stitches close to the edge of the fabric. Place the button, shank up, on the wrong side of the fabric and pull up gathering thread. Even out gathers and push back washer into place.*

 It is useful to make an extra button as a spare in case you lose one and have no fabric for a replacement.

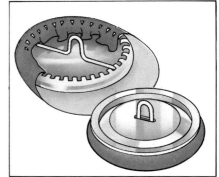

2 *If the button has a serrated edge on the reverse of the button front, ease the fabric over the prongs so that it covers the button front tautly and is held in place all around. Snap the back washer into place to cover raw edges.*

Covering curtain rings

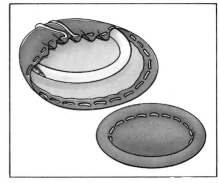

For buttons made from curtain rings, cut out a circle of fabric twice the width of the ring. Turn under raw edge and work running stitches close to the fold. Pull up the thread to gather the fabric over the ring. Fasten off. Topstitch close to the ring using backstitch.

Chinese ball buttons

Chinese ball buttons are a decorative fastening used with button loops or frog fastenings and look particularly appropriate on Oriental-style jackets, dresses and blouses. They can also be used as a feature on other garments, such as lingerie and baby clothes.

Chinese ball buttons can be made from a length of soft or corded tubing. Use soft tubing on lightweight fabrics and the corded type on heavier fabrics and outer garments. The diameter of the tubing should be less than half the diameter of the finished button. Use a narrow cord (about $\frac{1}{4}$in) for a small button, and larger cord for a larger button.

Decorative buttons

Make your buttons inspired and original by covering with exciting fabrics or decorating in an unusual way. Choose a single motif from a patterned fabric, or decorate plain fabrics with interesting stitch patterns, a simple appliqué shape, a lace motif, sequins or beads.

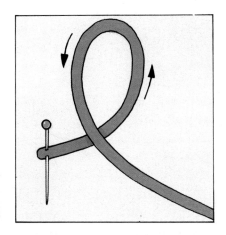

1 With the seam of the tubing facing downward, pin the end of the tubing to a piece of paper. Make the first loop in the direction shown.

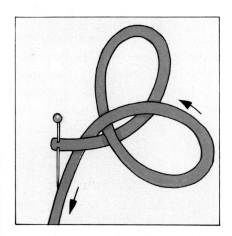

2 Make the second loop to the right of the first, looping from the bottom to the top and taking the free end under the end which is pinned.

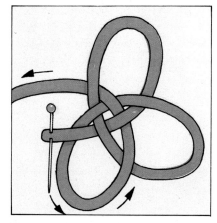

3 Make a third loop of the same size by taking the free end of the tubing back through the first two loops and weaving under and over as shown.

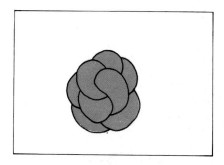

4 Tighten the loops carefully by easing them together until they are tightly woven. Trim the ends and sew securely to the underside.

Machine buttonholes

Machine buttonholes are quick and easy to do and give a neat, firm finish. They are suitable for most garments and fabrics and are always worked when the rest of the garment has been completed.

The way in which machine buttonholes are made will vary from model to model. All straight stitch machines need a special buttonhole attachment and feed plate to enable them to make buttonholes. Attachments are also available for zigzag machines which make buttonholing easier. Fully automatic machines will make buttonholes without attachments. Check the instructions for your own machine. carefully and practice stitch sizes on scraps of your fabric. A close, narrow zigzag is needed for the side of the buttonhole and double this width for the bars at each end.

Buttonhole size

The size of the buttonhole depends on the size of the button and is generally the diameter of the button, plus its thickness (usually about $\frac{1}{8}$in). To check that the buttonhole length is right for your button, cut a slit to this total measurement in a scrap of your fabric and try the button through it. It should not be so tight that the button has to be forced through or so loose that it will slip open.

Buttonhole position

The length and position of buttonholes are usually marked on the pattern. On a front opening the buttonholes are placed on the right side for a woman's garment and the left for a man's. Buttonholes are always on the left side of a back opening.

Buttonholes are usually used horizontally unless they are on a narrow opening such as a shirt band, when they are worked vertically. Horizontal buttonholes extend $\frac{1}{8}$in over the center line to allow for the shank of the button, and vertical buttonholes lie directly on it. There should always be approximately half the width of the button between the button and the edge of the opening.

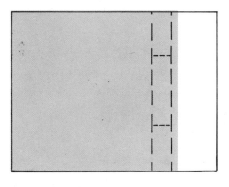

1 *Mark the position of the buttonholes on the right side of the garment with rows of basting stitches worked in a contrasting thread. Work two rows of basting parallel to the opening to mark the ends of the buttonholes, and baste between these to mark each individual buttonhole position.*

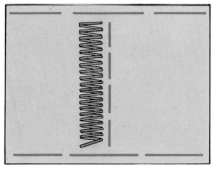

2 *To make a buttonhole using a zigzag machine without attachment, set the stitch length and width for a narrow, close zigzag and with the needle to the right, insert on center basted line. Work down left-hand side to end. Leave needle in fabric at outer edge.*

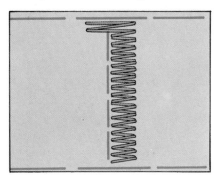

3 *Turn fabric around so that the second side of the buttonhole is now in line for stitching. Alter stitch width to larger size and work several stitchs across the end of the buttonhole, ending with the needle in the fabric at the outer edge of the buttonhole.*

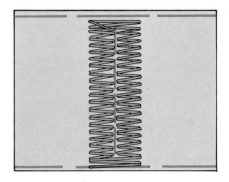

4 *Change sitch width to smaller size and work down the other side of buttonhole, leaving needle in the fabric at outer edge. Change stitch width to larger size and work several stitches to form second bar. Take ends through to wrong side and secure. Trim ends.*

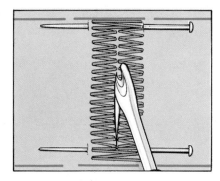

5 *Check the appearance and position of the finished buttonhole and then carefully slit between the lines of the stitching using a seam ripper, or cutting with the points of sharp scissors. Place a pin across each bar to avoid cutting through the stitches at each end.*

Hand-worked buttonholes

Hand-worked buttonholes are an alternative to machine buttonholes. They can be used on light and medium-weight fabrics, and are particularly suitable for fine fabrics and evening wear, as they have a more delicate appearance.

Like machine buttonholes, hand-worked buttonholes are made when the rest of the garment is finished. Horizontal buttonholes usaully have one bar end and one fan-shaped end worked so the bar is farthest from the opening and the fan shape next to it. Fan shapes can be worked at each end. Vertical buttonholes have two bar ends.

Positioning and marking

The same rules of positioning buttonholes apply as for machine buttonholes (see opposite). If positioning your own horizontal buttonholes, mark button position on center front line with tailor's chalk and draw buttonhole to extend $\frac{1}{8}$ in toward opening and then inward to required length. Mark vertical buttonholes an equal distance above and below the button position.

Preparing the buttonhole

Work small running stitches through all layers, stitching $\frac{1}{8}$ in from the marking at each side and directly across each end. This will reinforce the area when the buttonhole is cut and act as a guide to working even-length stitches.

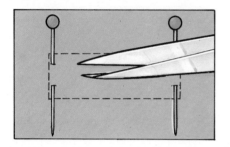

1 *Place a pin inside the stitching at each end of the buttonhole and cut through all layers at the center using the points of small sharp scissors or a seam ripper. Overcast the cut edges using matching thread.*

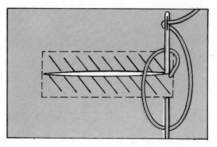

2 *Secure thread with a backstitch on wrong side. Bring needle through to right side. Insert needle through center slash and bring out on line of running stitches, looping thread around and under needle. Pull needle through to form a knot at the cut edge.*

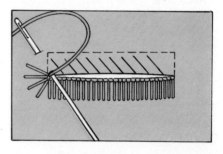

3 *Continue working from right to left, making even-length stitches closely together to give a firm buttonhole edge. At the end nearest the opening, work several evenly-spaced buttonhole stitches (or blanket stitch, as shown here) in a semi-circle to form a fan shape.*

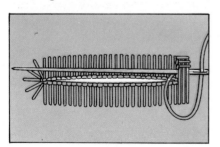

4 *Work other side as first. At the other end work several straight stitches across the total width of the buttonhole to form a bar. Bring needle back to the right-hand side of bar and work close blanket stitch along its length. Secure thread on wrong side.*

Bound buttonholes

Bound buttonholes are used on jackets and coats for a neat finish. They are made by stitching strips or patches of fabric to the buttonhole position, and cutting and turning them to the wrong side to bind the edges. This method is unsuitable for badly fraying fabrics or fabrics marked by machine basting. The fabric should also have enough depth in it to absorb the buttonhole without creating ridges.

Taken step by step, bound buttonholes are not difficult. They are made after the interfacing has been applied, but before the garment piece is joined to another. If there is no interfacing, cut a rectangle of interfacing the size of the patch and catch it to the wrong side of the garment piece before making the buttonhole. Very heavy interfacing (used on thick fabrics) is applied after making the buttonhole, to avoid stitching through unnecessary thickness.

Marking the buttonholes
Mark buttonholes with basting stitches, (see page 82), allowing $\frac{1}{4}$in over the center line for larger button shanks. Bound buttonholes must be at least $\frac{3}{4}$in

long to avoid lumpiness. They can be made wider or narrower than described by moving the machine basting farther from or closer to the buttonhole center line, increasing the width of the patch if necessary. Patches for bound buttonholes can be cut on the bias. This makes a soft buttonhole which is easy to do up over a button, but the pieces are more awkward to handle while making the buttonhole.

Marking the stitching lines
The main difficulty with these buttonholes is the exact placing of the lines for stitching. It is wise to check the spacing of the lines at each stage. It may help to cut out part of the pattern piece, including the buttonholes, center line and adjacent edges, on graph paper. Make the pattern in reverse, aligning and marking the buttonholes and stitching lines as well as the center line, and attaching more graph paper if needed for the length. Pin this pattern to the wrong side of the fabric and stitch from the wrong side along the stitching lines, otherwise proceeding as usual. Tear the paper away carefully before cutting the buttonhole, saving it for use on the facing. The position of the openings in the facing may be found using the graph paper or by placing the garment and facing together and placing pins through both layers from the right side at each corner of the buttonhole.

Making the buttonholes

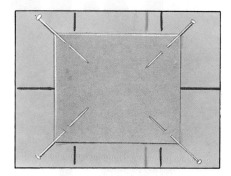

1 *For each buttonhole cut a rectangle of fabric on the straight grain, 2in deep and 1in longer than the buttonhole. With right sides together, center the patch over the buttonhole and pin it in place.*

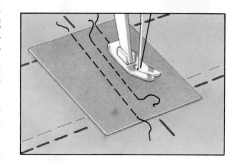

2 *With a normal stitch length, stitch along the center line to the exact length of the buttonhole. With a long stitch length, stitch ¼in each side of the center line, along the whole length of the patch.*

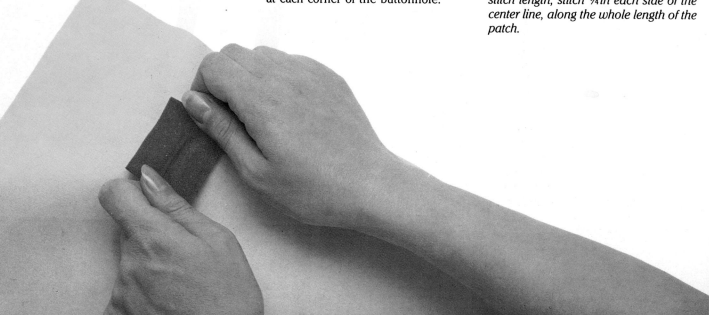

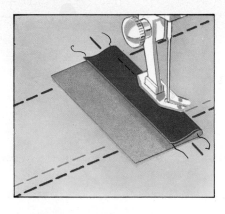

3 Press down one side of the patch along the machine basting line. With a very small stitch (about 1/16 in or less), stitch halfway between basting and central stitching lines (1/8 in from each), to exact length of buttonhole.

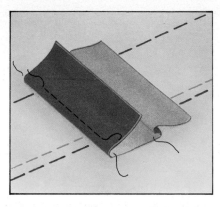

4 At the ends of the stitching bring the threads through to one side and knot. Press up the other side of the patch and stitch as before. Check the position of the stitching lines by measuring.

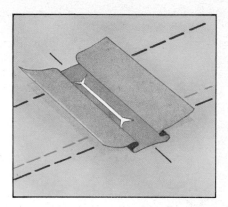

5 Cut along the center line to within 1/4–3/8 in of each end of buttonhole, through both layers of the fabric. Cut diagonally into the corners and remove the machine basting threads.

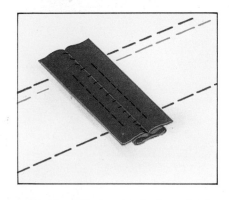

6 Gently pull the patch through the hole and press. On the right side baste the lips of the buttonhole together with diagonal stitches and slipstitch the rest of the folds together on the wrong side.

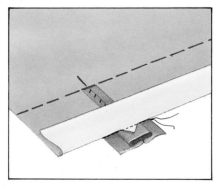

7 With right side up, fold back fabric to expose the end of the buttonhole patch with the triangle on top. Secure by stitching across it several times with a small stitch. Repeat at the other end of the buttonhole.

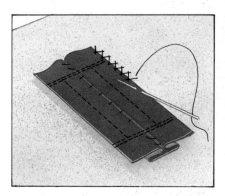

8 Trim the patch to 1/4 in from stitching. If a heavy interfacing is used, apply it now, cutting out a rectangle for each buttonhole. Arrange under the edges of the fabric at the wrong side of the buttonhole. Tack patch to the interfacing with herringbone stitch.

Finishing the facing

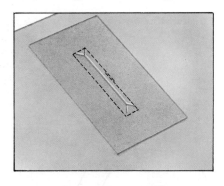

1 Cut a patch in lining fabric 1 1/2 in wide and 1 in longer than the buttonhole. With right sides together, center the patch over the buttonhole marking. Using a small stitch, stitch a rectangle 1/8 in to each side of the center line and across the ends of the buttonhole. Cut the center as before.

2 Turn the patch through to the wrong side of the facing with the stitching on the edge of the fold. Press. When the facing is in place, slipstitch the edges of the facing opening to the edges of the buttonhole in the garment.

3 A quick way of finishing buttonholes in a facing is to cut along the center line, tuck raw edges to wrong side and slipstitch to the back of the buttonhole.

Fastenings

Hooks and eyes, snaps and nylon tape are all means of securing overlapping openings. Usually the design suggests which fastening to use, although in some cases they are interchangeable. Use small hooks and eyes or snaps on sheer or fine fabrics, and larger sizes on heavyweight fabrics.

Hooks and eyes

Hooks and eyes are made in various sizes and styles to suit all weights of fabric and the opening on which they are used, such as necklines and waistbands. Eyes are made of either loops or bars. Use a straight bar eye when the edges of the closure overlap and a round eye when the edges of the closure just meet.

Snaps

Snaps are used for neck and shoulder fastenings, for openings on sheer fabrics or where buttonholes are impractical. They give a neat flat closure.

There are two types of snaps: those which are sewn on and those which are bought in kit form and applied with a special tool. These are use on children's clothes and sportswear and are easily and quickly applied following the instructions with the kit.

Nylon tape

Nylon tape is a strip fastening that sticks when both halves are pressed together. It is excellent for fastening buckle-less belts, waistbands in wrapped or adjustable-waist garments, jacket fronts and cuffs and can replace almost any fastening. It is, however, too bulky to use in place of a zipper in a dress, skirt or pants placket or in lightweight garments.

Nylon tape can be bought by the yard or in packaged lengths and comes in several basic colors. As it does not fray, it can be cut to size and applied by slipstitching, machine stitching invisibly, or topstitching to the garment. When sewing nylon tape to the garment by hand, it may help to run the thread through beeswax first to strengthen it.

 Use a fine needle for sewing hooks and eyes and snaps in place, so that it will pass through the small holes.

Hook and eye

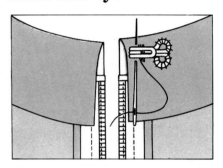

1 *Where the edges of a garment meet, position a hook ⅛in in from one edge. Take a few small stitches under the hook to secure the thread and overcast or buttonhole stitch around each hole, making sure stitches do not show on the right side. Carry the needle to the shank of hook and take several stitches across this end to hold it securely.*

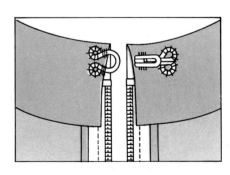

2 *Position a round eye on the opposite edge, so that the loop overlaps by ⅛in. Secure the thread with a few small stitches and overcast or buttonhole stitch around each hole and then across the side of the eye to hold it securely in place.*

Nylon tape

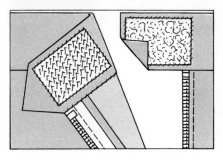

To slipstitch nylon tape in position use single thread. Separate the strip and place the soft side on the right side of underlap at opening and pin in place. Work small hemming stitches all around. Pin firm side to wrong side of overlap and sew in place in the same way as before.

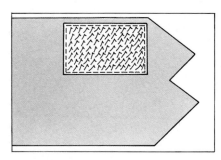

To machine stitch nylon tape invisibly in place, separate the two sides of tape. Before making waistband, pin the firm side to the inner side of waistband or opening overlap. Stitch all around and complete the waistband or opening. Stitch the soft side of the fastening directly to the underlap, through all thicknesses.

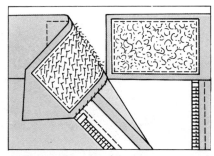

When topstitching nylon tape in place, complete the opening or wrap first, and then pin and baste the soft side of the tape to the underlap and the firm side to the overlap to correspond. Machine stitch around the edges of both pieces, through all thicknesses.

Snaps

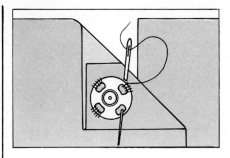

1 *Secure the thread with a few back-stitches on the wrong side of the overlap. Sew the ball half of the snap in position by overcasting through each hole three or four times and carrying the thread under the snap from one hole to the next. Fasten off securely, making sure stitches do not show on the right side.*

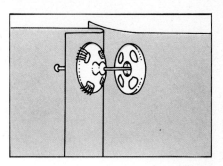

2 *Position the socket half of the snap on the right side of the underlap to correspond. Find the position by placing a pin through the center of both the attached ball half and the socket half of the snap and closing the opening. Stitch in place by overcasting as before.*

WORKBOX

Zippers

A standard medium-weight zipper with metal teeth for general use. Insert before fitting waistband.

Lightweight nylon zipper for dresses and skirts have the advantage of being inconspicuous.

An invisible zipper is used with fine fabrics on tailored clothes, to avoid spoiling the line of the garment.

For pants and active sportswear a heavier-weight zipper is desirable. Some are intended to be visible.

Inserting a zipper

Zippers are a simple-to-use fastening and, taken step by step, they are easy to put in as well. This method is ideal for straight seams such as center front or back seams, and for use with bulky fabrics. The pattern will tell you how long a zipper you need, but check this measurement if you have made any alterations to the length of the pattern. The length of a zipper is measured from the bottom stop to the top of the teeth. The opening should be the length of the zipper plus $\frac{1}{8}$-$\frac{1}{4}$in and top seam allowance. Remember that the opening will seem slightly shorter when the zipper is in, and needs to be long enough for you to put the garment on and take it off without straining the zipper.

Different weights of zipper are available with teeth made of metal, nylon or polyester. Choose a zipper in the appropriate color and weight for the fabric. Generally nylon and polyester zippers are suitable for dresses and skirts in light and medium-weight fabrics, and metal zippers for pants and heavyweight fabrics. Make sure that the zipper opens without sticking before you put it in. Never cut the zipper tape. Fold it back, with a miter if necessary. Always press a zipper with a press cloth.

Preparing the opening
You need seam allowances of at least $\frac{5}{8}$in to insert a zipper comfortably, and on fraying or bulky fabrics allow about $\frac{3}{4}$in. Bias or stretchy seams need special attention to prevent stretching. Baste the opening edges firmly before applying the zipper, or staystitch with a long machine stitch.

Inserting the zipper
Use a zipper foot if you have one, and stitch both sides of the zipper in the same direction. This is preferable, as the fabric can look pulled if you stitch all around in one movement. Be careful not to break your needle by forgetting to align it correctly with the zipper foot. If you cannot position the needle to either

side of the foot (or the foot to either side of the needle), sew in zipper by starting at the top, stitching down one side, across the bottom and up the other side. If you have trouble stitching past the slider, leave the needle in the fabric, raise the foot and move the slider up or down. Lower foot; resume stitching.

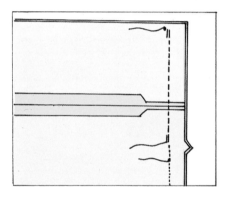

1 With right sides together, match notches and dots and pin, baste and stitch the seam to the opening, finishing the ends securely. Press the stitching. Baste the opening along the seamline, trimming any interfacing or seam allowances that meet it, then press the seam open.

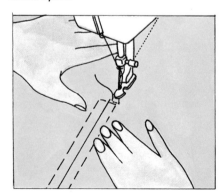

3 With the needle on the left side of the zipper foot and the right side of the garment facing, stitch from the center of the base of the zipper, along the right side, to the top. Change the needle position to the other side of the foot and stitch the other side, beginning at the bottom of the zipper as before.

 Most zippers have an obvious raised line on the tape about $\frac{1}{4}$in from the center of the teeth. Use this as your guideline when basting and stitching the zipper in place.

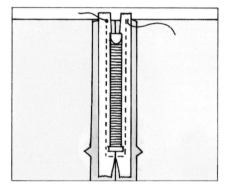

2 Place zipper face down on wrong side of fabric, aligning center of zipper teeth with basted seam. Pin from the bottom with the stop just above stitching of the seam. This should bring the top to $\frac{1}{8}$-$\frac{1}{4}$in from top seamline. Take care not to stretch the zipper as you pin. Baste all around, $\frac{1}{4}$in from the center.

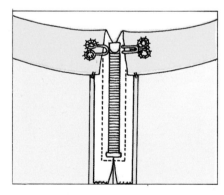

4 Secure the ends of the thread, then remove all the basting. If there is a facing, fold it down and back from the zipper and stitch to tapes to avoid catching it in zipper teeth. Catch stitch lower ends of tapes to seam allowances. With a collar and/or facing, sew a hook and eye above the zipper.

FINISHINGS
Invisible hemming

All garments, however simple or complicated, need a well-turned hem, and its appearance really can make or mar the finished look. Here is one simple basic method which is suitable for most garments and fabrics.

Leveling

If cut accurately, most hemlines will be level. If not, use a hem-marker or get a friend to use a tape measure and insert pins in a straight line for you. Skirts cut on the bias should be left to drop and can then be evened off. Full-curved hems should be $\frac{3}{4}$–1in deep, average dress or skirt hems $1\frac{1}{2}$in, coats 2–3in. If the garment is too long, trim off the excess fabric, leaving the hem depth, which is usually specified in the pattern instructions.

 Avoid making hems too deep; it makes it difficult to ease the fullness of the hem allowance and is one of the main causes of lumpy hems.

Finishing

Avoid folding the top edge under to finish except on narrow machine-stitched hems. The most durable way to finish the edge is with zigzag stitch, but avoid stretching the edge. If this occurs, try three-step zigzag (tricot), or zigzag $\frac{3}{8}$in in from the edge and trim back to this stitching. Fairly non-fray fabrics can just be reinforced with a row of straight stitching about $\frac{3}{8}$in from the edge, and then trimmed back to the stitching line with pinking shears.

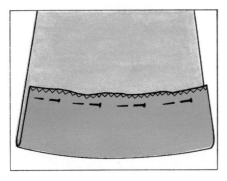

1 *Finish hem edge and press. Fold up hem, keeping an even curve at the fold. Pin about $\frac{5}{8}$in down from top edge, gently easing in fullness. Avoid forming pleats in the hem; if impossible cut the hem allowance shorter. Baste on pin line.*

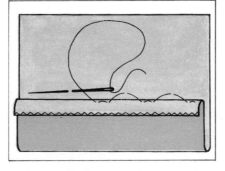

2 *Fold back top edge. Start and finish with backstitches into hem. Stitch into garment just above fold, taking up only one thread or part of a thick thread.*

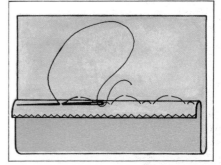

3 *Leaving stitches loose so that no indentations show on right side, stitch into fold of hem Backstitch into hem in same place: this locking stitch prevents the hem from undoing if snagged.*

 If you have difficulty matching thread with the fabric of your choice, pick a deeper shade to go with solid-color material or with one of the dark colors of a print.

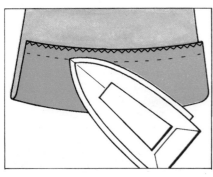

4 *On wrong side only steam-press to just below finished edge. Prevent marks on stitching line by slipping edge of iron under top edge of hem (right) to press.*

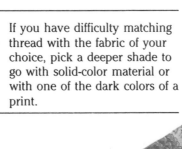

Bias binding

Bias bound edges are an attractive way of finishing a garment and are easy to do. Make your own bias binding by cutting and joining bias strips (see page 92) to finish your garment with a binding which matches the main fabric exactly, or to make a contrast binding in fabric of the same weight. Purchased bias bindings are an easy alternative to cutting your own, and are available in a variety of widths, and cotton and satin finishes. Use a contrasting color or a different texture to emphasize the edge, but remember to choose a fabric which is compatible with the garment fabric for washing.

Preparing the binding

If you are making your own binding, decide on the finished width required, double this and add $\frac{1}{2}$in for seam allowances. Cut and join bias strips to the required length, allowing for joinings and shrinkage. Shrink by steam pressing. (Purchased bias binding is pre-shrunk.) Fold the binding in half, wrong sides together, and press. Open out and press $\frac{1}{2}$in seam allowances to wrong side along each edge.

If you are binding a curved edge, shape the binding by steam pressing before applying it and staystitch the curved edge.

Stitching the binding

No seam allowance is needed on the garment edges which are being bound. Purchased bias bindings have the raw edges turned in almost to the center fold, so when you align the raw edges of the garment and binding, the binding is automatically placed correctly. On other, especially wider, bindings, place the crease of the binding almost half the width of the binding from the raw edge of the garment and take extra care to keep this stitching line straight. By pinning, but not basting, the binding in place before stitching, you will unconsciously stretch it a little as you stitch, which helps the final look. However, basting is advisable on curves. Avoid joining the binding as far as possible, and place necessary joinings at side seams, center back seams or somewhere inconspicuous.

Slipstitch method

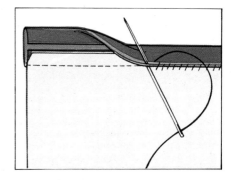

Unfold one edge of binding. With raw edges even, pin binding to fabric, right sides together. Pin and stitch in crease of fold. Fold binding over raw edges to wrong side and hem folded edge along previous stitching.

Machine method

Pin and stitch binding in place as before. Fold binding over raw edges to wrong side and baste folded edge in place just below previous stitching line. Machine stitch from right side in hollow of first stitching.

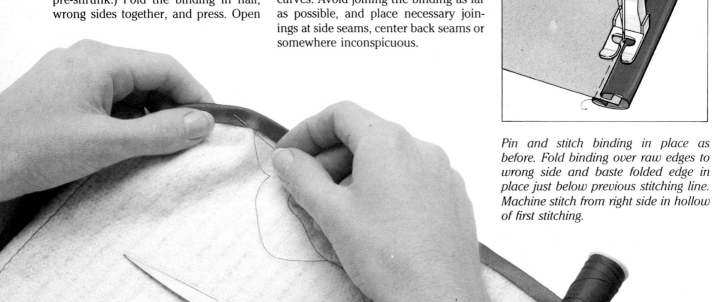

Topstitch method

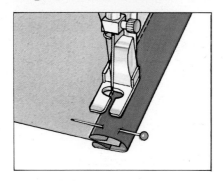

Unfold one edge of binding and with raw edges even, pin binding to fabric with right side of binding to wrong side of fabric. Pin and stitch in crease of fold. Fold binding over raw edges to right side to cover previous stitching line. Pin and topstitch along edge of binding from right side.

Outward corners

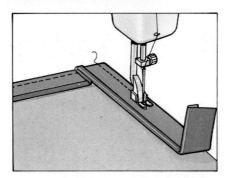

Stitch binding to one edge, ending the stitching where the seamlines meet at corner. Cut and knot threads. Place binding in line with next edge, forming a diagonal fold at corner. Stitch from raw edge down this side. Fold binding over raw edge to wrong side, forming a similar fold at corner, slipstitch or machine stitch from right side.

Inward corners

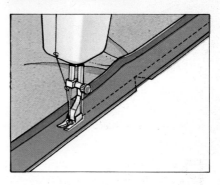

Reinforce the corner with small machine stitches. Clip to stitching. Stitch binding to edge as usual and leave needle in fabric at corner. Raise the presser foot, straighten the fabric to align it with the binding. Lower the foot and continue stitching. Fold binding over raw edge to wrong side, forming a fold at the corner on both sides. Complete as usual.

Making bias strips

Bias strips can be cut of self or contrasting fabric to give a variety of finishes, both decorative and practical. The cut on the true bias is used because this is the direction of greatest elasticity within a fabric, making the final strips smooth, not buckled, around curves. Fabrics vary in the amount they stretch on the bias and you should check that your fabric has sufficient give in it for your purpose. Bias strips can be cut just off the true bias to economize on fabric. This works well as long as the strips have enough stretch, and the fabric is not checked or striped or otherwise patterned to show the irregular cut. Regular-patterned fabrics need to be straightened if they are off-grain (see page 20), before cutting the strips, in order to maintain the regularity of the pattern.

Deciding the width
The width of a bias strip is normally twice the finished width plus seam allowances of at least ¼in, but this may vary with their purpose. Strips need to be stretched a little as they are pressed; otherwise they hold some slack, which leads to puckers later. This means they lose some width and may need to be cut fractionally wider to allow for this. Remember, too, to allow extra length for seams and finishing off the ends when cutting the strips.

Making joinings
Joinings can look conspicuous, so cut long strips to minimize them and place necessary joinings where they will be least noticeable on the garment. The ends of the strips are cut on the straight grain, and should be all on the lengthwise, or all on the crosswise grain. It is simple to cut the strips and

An alternative method of finding the true bias is to fold the corner across the fabric, bringing the selvage onto a crosswise thread. Mark the diagonal fold with chalk or a basting thread and measure parallel lines from it.

Cutting the strips

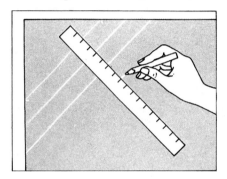

Find the true bias of the fabric by measuring equal distances on two adjoining edges and joining these two points. Mark the required width of strip from this line, measuring at right angles to it, and join points to make a parallel line. Mark as many strips as you need. Cut strips with sharp scissors and press, stretching slightly as you do so.

Making a diagonal sleeve

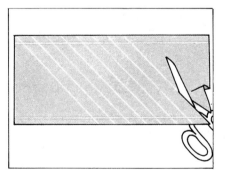

1 *Mark the lines for the strips on the wrong side of a rectangle of fabric as before, together with a seamline for joining at top and bottom. Cut off corners of unmarked fabric. With right side inside, pin the seamlines together matching A to B and Y to Z, so that the width of a strip overlaps at each end.*

then join them in one or two carefully placed seams, but if you need a long strip it is quicker to use the diagonal sleeve method shown below.

Joining the strips

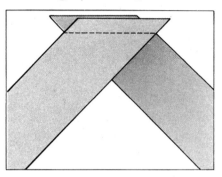

Cut the ends on the straight (lengthwise or crosswise) grain of the fabric and place the strips right sides together, with ends even. The sides of the strips should meet at the stitching line, about ¼in from the ends. Pin and stitch. Press seam open. Trim off projecting corners of seam allowances. Repeat until you have the required length.

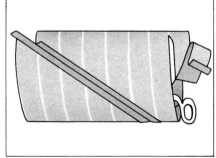

2 *Stitch along the seamline and press the seam open. With sharp scissors cut along the marked line, beginning at A and continuing around the cylinder until you reach Z. Press as before, stretching the strip slightly to remove the slack. This gives one long strip.*

Lining and underlining

Lining and underlining improve the hang of a garment, prolong its life and reduce the creases that form through wear.

Lining

Lining neatens the inside of a garment and helps the garment to keep its shape. It also makes rough fabrics more comfortable to wear and helps the garment to slip on and off more easily. Choose the lining carefully, using a smooth, firm and crease-resistant fabric of the same or a lighter weight than the main garment fabric.

Underlining

Underlining is used to support and strengthen loosely-woven fabric and prevent stretching. It is used as a backing for sheer and lace fabrics and helps prevent seams and darts from showing through to the right side. Lightweight fabrics are often underlined in self-fabric, but avoid underlining polyester fabric with polyester, as this creates static. Drapes, folds, gathered sleeves pleats and knits are spoiled by underlining.

Choose an underlining with the same washing/cleaning requirements as the main garment fabric and choose a color which will not change the color of the outer fabric if it shows through. Fabrics sold as underlining are light to medium in weight and have soft and crisp finishes, so choose one to give the desired effect. Use woven underlining on woven fabric and cut both on the same grain of the fabric.

Methods of underlining

There are two methods of underlining. The main garment pieces can be cut in fabric and underlining, placed wrong sides together and treated as one piece, or they can be handled separately until the darts have been made and then handled as one. The first method reinforces seams and darts and prevents details from showing through to the right side. The second gives a neater finish to the inside and prevents seams – but not darts – from showing on the right side. The first method (shown here) is the more usual of the two.

As the pieces are stitched with the underlining uppermost, the pattern markings can be transferred to the underlining only, but it is safer to tailor tack through both layers. On slippery fabrics it may help to stitch both layers together along the center of the dart before stitching the dart itself, and on heavier fabrics it may help to slash the underlining along the center of the dart and ease it apart a little. Seams must be finished. Consider trimming the main fabric seam allowance and binding the raw edge with the untrimmed underlining seam allowance. Stitch facings to the underlining only at the seams, not all the way around.

Underlining

1 *Cut out fabric and underlining pieces from the same pattern piece. Place wrong side of main fabric to wrong side of underlining, replace the pattern and tailor tack the markings through both layers. Baste layers together around edges and through center of darts. Continue to assemble garment, handling each piece as one fabric.*

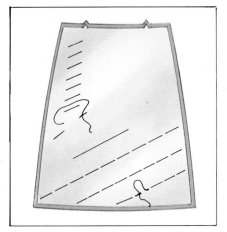

2 *On large pieces, baste diagonally in rows down the length of the garment with the grain of the fabric and underlining parallel to avoid twisting. Bias-cut pieces may need rows of basting 2in apart. With underlining uppermost and a thread that matches the main fabric, stitch parallel to the grain, catching one or two threads in each stitch.*

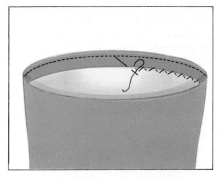

3 *To finish the hem, make a row of running stitches just inside the hemline through both layers of fabric. Turn up the hem, pulling up the stitches slightly to ease in fabric if necessary. Fold under or finish the raw edge, then hem to the underlining only. Avoid deep hems, especially on flared skirts.*

Lining a skirt

1 To assemble the lining, cut out, stitch and finish the seams in the same way as the main skirt pieces, leaving an opening for the zipper ¼in longer than the skirt opening. Machine stitch the hem, making it 1in shorter than the final skirt length.

Lining a skirt

The method of attaching a lining varies from garment to garment. Lining a skirt is relatively simple. The main pieces are cut in lining fabric and assembled in the same way as the skirt. A half lining can be made by cutting pieces to just below the seat area. Lining pieces are usually cut on the same grain as the skirt pieces, although a bias-cut skirt may have a lining cut on the straight grain and full skirts may have straight or A-line shaped linings, with perhaps a ruffle at the bottom to hold out the skirt. Whatever the shape or cut, the method of inserting the lining is the same. Any alterations to the skirt must be made to the lining as well, so fit the skirt before cutting out the lining.

Remember to leave a zipper opening on the right-hand side of the lining for a left-hand opening in the skirt. Most lining fabrics fray, so finish the seam allowances by turning under the edges and stitching along the fold. On tight skirts, make the lining about ⅛in tighter on the hips at each side to help reduce seating. If you are unsure about the length of the skirt and delay hemming the lining until it is in the skirt, be careful not to catch the main fabric while stitching. French tacks between skirt and lining at the seams prevent the lining from twisting around.

Pressing a lined skirt is more difficult

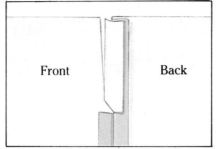

Front   Back

2 To make an opening for a lapped zipper, press the seam open, then clip the front seam allowance to the stitching and press toward the back. Remove this portion of the seam allowance by clipping diagonally to ½in from the top of the stitching and then cutting from the waist to top of clip.

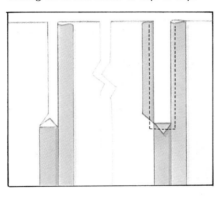

3 To finish opening, clip diagonally from the edge of the front lining to ½in in from the edge to match the first clip, as shown. Fold back the front edge and flap at the base of the opening to wrong side of front and stitch close to folded edge.

4 To attach the lining to the skirt, place lining and skirt pieces wrong sides together and pin and baste together around waist. Fit. Place waistband and skirt right sides together and complete as usual. Hem the lining to the zipper tape, clear of the teeth.

Lining pleats

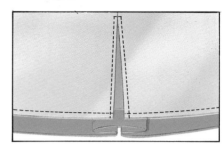

For a single pleat, make the lining with a seam in the place of the center fold of the pleat. Stitch the seam from the waist to the top of the pleat and press open. Turn remaining seam allowances to wrong side along opening and stitch.

Partial lining

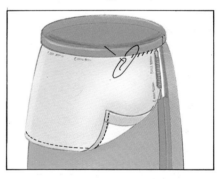

To reduce seating, add a partial lining to the back of the skirt. Cut lining to just below hip level, using skirt pattern piece, and stitch darts. If possible cut with the bottom edge on the selvage to avoid hemming. Turn under the seam allowances at waist and side edges and hem to the finished skirt.

with French tacks at the hemline, and is awkward around the zipper. Overcome this by stitching the lining around the zipper opening to hold back the seam allowance, but not hemming it to the zipper tape.

The lining can be put in after the skirt is finished by assembling as usual, turning under the seam allowance at the waist edge and hemming at the waist and around the zipper. This method makes relining easier. It can also be used for partial linings (lining the back only to reduce seating, lining the front only to reduce creases, or lining around the top of pleats in a pleated skirt). Usually the time and effort involved make a complete lining as worthwhile as a partial one.

DIFFERENT FABRICS
Knits

Knit fabrics – as the name indicates – are knitted, not woven. Most have some degree of stretch, usually with more stretch across the width and a lesser amount down the length. They come in a variety of weights.

Double knit
The heavier double knits, often wool or acrylic, are used mainly for jackets, skirts and pants. They have far less stretch than finer knits and, provided a small stitch and polyester thread are used, they can usually be treated in the same way as woven fabrics of similar weight.

Bonded knits
These have another fabric, usually knitted but sometimes woven, bonded to the wrong side. This often removes most of the stretch factor.

Cotton and fine synthetic knits
These types are usually soft and pliable and will drape beautifully. They are often quite stretchy, especially across the width. Seam allowances may roll and edges are stretched by finishing, necessitating special techniques for good results.

Velour and stretch terry cloth
All knit fabrics are technically one-way fabrics because each knitted stitch has a top and bottom and looks different when reversed. Occasionally this can cause a color disparity even on fine knits. However most fine knits can be cut either way up without any noticeable difference. Velours, terry cloth and heavier knit fabrics must be cut as one-way fabrics.

Raschel knit
This is an open lace-like knitted fabric, usually polyester, used mainly for dresses, tops and soft jackets.

Interfacing
Choose a soft, pliable interfacing so that interfaced parts, while losing their stretch, maintain a softness compatible with the rest of the garment.

Taping
Taping seams prevents seams from stretching and is sometimes necessary on shoulder seams with heavier knits. It is not usually used on lighter weights, as the fabric on each side of the seam can still stretch, causing the rigid taped seam to look puckered.

Knit samples, left to right: bouclé knit, striped stretch terry cloth, plain double knit, fine patterned cotton knit and velour.

Fastenings
Because of the stretch factor, knit fabrics are particularly suited to styles that do not need fastenings. Avoid zippers and buttonholes wherever you can. Where they are unavoidable choose a lightweight zipper and take care not to stretch the fabric when inserting it. Always interface buttonhole areas and, if possible, work buttonholes vertically in knit fabric.

Needles
Use a medium to fine needle (14-11) according to fabric weight, and polyester thread, which is more resistant to snapping than cotton. Fine polyester knits cause some machines to skip stitches. Avoid this by using a ball-point needle.

Stitching

For seams, use a slightly smaller stitch than usual (14 stitches per inch) to help prevent seams from snapping, and stretch the fabric slightly as you stitch. Always test technique first on spare fabric. Alternatively, a very narrow zigzag stitch may be used where the seam will be under stress, such as in tracksuits and sportswear. However this does not give such a good stitch line and is more suited to velour and terry cloth, where it will not show.

Machine stretch stitch is a very strong stitch which is good for seams that are under stress. However, it does tend to stretch and buckle the seam on lightweight knits.

Finishing

To prevent stretching the edge while zigzag stitching, work the stitching a little way in from the edge and then trim the edge back to the stitching. Use a medium width zigzag stitch or preferably a three-step zigzag stitch (tricot) which gives a flatter finish. Press flat before trimming.

Knit seams

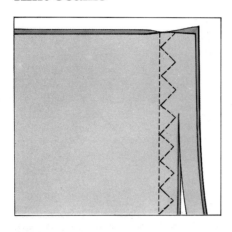

Stitch the seam, then finish by zigzag stitching both the seam allowances together immediately next to stitching. Press stitching flat. Trim the seam allowance back to stitching and press seam to one side.

Knit hems

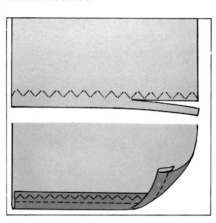

Finish by zigzag stitching a little in from edge. Press stitching flat. Trim edge back to stitching. Turn and stitch a deep hem in the usual way, or fold ⅝in to wrong side and topstitch ⅜in from the fold for a narrow hem.

Band finishes

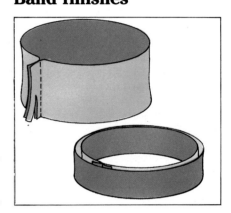

1 *Band finishes are quick and easy, and give a professional finish to sleeves and necklines on knit fabrics. Make band smaller than edge to be finished (slightly smaller on sleeves and more so for round necks). Stitch band to form a ring, trim and press seam open. Fold band in half with right side outside.*

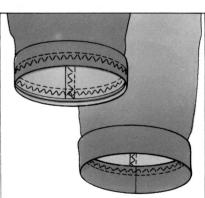

2 *Place the band around the right side of the edge to be finished, with the raw edges even, stretching the band to fit. Stitch seam, then zigzag stitch all the seam allowances together just next to stitching. Trim fabric to zigzag stitching and fold band away from garment.*

Pile fabrics

Velvet, velveteen and corduroy share the characteristic of having a raised texture, or pile, formed by an additional thread in the weaving process. Velvet is the most luxurious of these fabrics. Once made of silk, it is now most often of rayon or another synthetic fiber. As it tends to be slippery, it is best avoided by the less experienced dressmaker. Velveteen is a similar fabric made of cotton. Some velveteens have a thick, rich pile; others are rather flat; but they are all relatively easy to work with, provided you observe a few simple rules. Corduroy is also made of cotton, although cotton-synthetic blends are now fairly common. It comes in a variety of weights, from fine pin-wale corduroy to heavy, wide-wale types.

Choosing a pattern

Simple styles are best for deep pile velvets and velveteens. Avoid too many seams, topstitching, pleats, folds and tucks. Lightweight velveteen and corduroy can have a little more ambitious styling, although pleats are still best avoided.

Try to choose a pattern which specifies velvet, or at least one which has a "with nap" layout. The pile of these fabrics looks lighter one way than the other, so the pattern pieces must all be positioned in the same direction on the fabric.

If your chosen design does not include a special layout for napped fabric, buy the pattern first so that you can calculate how much extra fabric will be needed. To do this, first make any adjustments to the pattern lengths, then lay out all the relevant pieces, all facing in one direction on the right grain, within an area with the same width as the velvet. Measure the total length to arrive at the amount required, then make a rough sketch of the layout before refolding the pieces.

Cutting out

First determine which way up to cut the fabric. For the richest, darkest color effect the pile should smooth upward on all pieces, from hem to neckline. To find the pile direction lay the fabric right side up, on a flat surface and stroke along the length with the flat of your hand. The surface of the fabric will feel smooth when stroking with the pile and slightly rough against it. Mark the "top" end of the length with a contrasting thread to remind you which way the pattern has to be placed.

On some pile fabrics it is easier to cut out from a single layer, but if you do this remember to turn over all the relevant pattern pieces to obtain the second piece, or the other half of the pattern (usually shown by shading on the cutting layouts).

Pin sparingly and always within the seam allowances to prevent marking. Use sharp dressmaking shears when cutting out and transfer the pattern markings with tailor's tacks using a soft, fine thread, such as basting thread or silk, and a fine needle.

Stitching

Always baste the seams before stitching, using small basting stitches and taking the occasional backstitch to keep the basting firm. Fit the basted garment before machine stitching to avoid alterations and unpicking, as stitch marks are very difficult to remove.

For stitching velveteen or corduroy, use mercerized cotton – No. 40 or 50, depending on fabric weight – or cotton-wrapped polyester. Fine polyester or silk thread is suitable for velvet. Stitch with a fine to medium needle, size 9 to 14 (9 or 11 is most appropriate for velvet) and a stitch length of 10-12 stitches per inch.

Always make a test seam on a spare piece of fabric, and stitch in the direction of the pile. If the layers move away from each other as you stitch, despite careful basting, insert a strip of tissue paper between the layers, then baste and stitch, tearing away the paper afterward. Alternatively slacken the presser foot pressure slightly, if it is adjustable.

To remove basting stitches, clip the thread at intervals along the seam and pull out short lengths. Avoid pulling out long lengths of thread as this may rip through the pile and mark it.

Pressing
Method 1

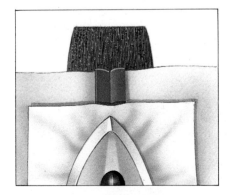

To press velvets that mark easily, lay the garment face down on a needleboard, cover the work with a press cloth and steam press.

Method 2

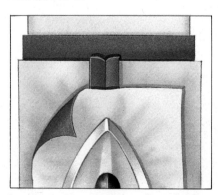

Place a spare piece of velvet face up on the ironing board and arrange the velvet garment face down over it. Cover wrong side of garment with a press cloth or another piece of velvet and steam press.

Pressing

Test press a spare piece of velvet with the iron on a setting suitable for the type of velvet you are using. Some of the sturdier types of velveteen will withstand pressing on the wrong side, with the garment placed directly on the ironing board. Most velvets, however, cannot be pressed in the normal way, as the pile would be crushed, resulting in shiny patches. Instead, press the fabric over a needleboard, or spare piece of velvet, or steam, as described below. Never press over pins, which cut into the pile.

Interfacing

Use sew-in interfacing rather than iron-on interfacing, unless working with the sturdier corduroys or some velveteens, which can withstand the hot temperature needed to fuse the interfacing to the fabric.

Finishing

Velvet frays badly, so all raw edges should be finished as soon as possible. Edges can be finished by zigzag stitching, overcasting closely by hand, or binding with a bias binding. Never use pinking shears.

Fastenings

Avoid buttonholes unless working with lightweight corduroy or velveteen, which are thin enough to take them. Substitute thread loops, frog fastenings or zippers. Zippers are easier to insert by hand, using prick stitch.

Care of fabric

Most pile fabrics should be dry cleaned unless care instructions state otherwise. Corduroy can be hand or machine washed on a short cycle. Avoid wringing, which would crush the pile, and drip dry. Hang the garment on a padded hanger and try not to crush in an overcrowded closet. If creases appear, hang the garment in a steamy room so that they fall out.

Steaming

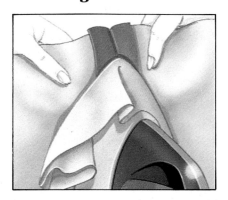

To open seams of velvet garments without pressing, finger press the seam open, then hold the wrong side up to a hot iron covered with a well-wrung wet cloth. Take care not to handle the velvet too much while it is still damp.

Attaching interfacing

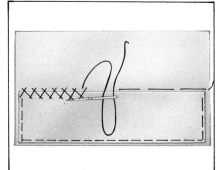

To eliminate bulk on a double cuff, cut sew-in interfacing to half the depth. Mark the fold line as a guide for positioning the interfacing and catch edge down with herringbone stitch. Always trim close to stitching on seams.

Binding raw edges

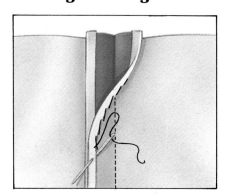

To bind raw edges before they fray too badly, stitch bias strips of thin silky fabric or bias binding to the right side of the seam allowance, turn to the underside, fold under raw edge and hem in place.

Sheer fabrics

There are many different types of sheer fabric. Some, such as chiffon, georgette, organza and lace, are soft and delicate, while others, such as dotted swiss, organdy and net, are crisper. All require a little extra care when sewing to ensure success.

Choosing the pattern
As sheer fabrics are fine and transparent, seams and darts will show through to the right side and spoil the look of the garment, so choose a pattern with as little shaping as possible and use gathering, ruffles and soft pleats to give fullness and flare.

Cutting out
Before laying out the fabric, make sure your table is clean and smooth to avoid marking and snagging the fabric. If your cutting table is shiny and the fabric slips, cover the table with an old sheet or large tablecloth. Pin pattern pieces in place within the seam allowance, using extra fine steel pins known as pleating pins. Cut out with sharp dressmaking shears and use tailor's tacks to mark pattern markings. Chalk and dressmaker's carbon paper can show through to the right side and are sometimes difficult to remove.

Interfacing
Where interfacings are necessary, use the lightest possible sew-in interfacing. If you want a completely sheer effect, use net or organdy.

Stitching
Use very fine needles for hand and machine stitching. Machine needle no. 9 is the best size for most sheers. Use silk thread for silk sheers, polyester for synthetic fabrics and blends, and fine mercerized cotton (no. 50) for cotton sheers such as organdy, voile and batiste. Before stitching the main garment, test the stitch length on a scrap of your fabric: 12-15 stitches to an inch is the recommended size. If the fabric puckers, place a sheet of tissue paper under fabric and stitch through layers. Gently tear away paper after stitching.

Seams
Seams should be finished neatly so they show as little as possible on the right side. Enclosed seams such as French seams and self-bound seams are ideal, although the former can only be used on straight or slightly shaped seams and are not suitable for armhole curves. Double-stitched seams can also be used. Avoid facings wherever you can, and finish raw edges at neck and cuffs with binding.

Fastening
Lightweight snaps are ideal for lapped openings, and have the advantage of being completely hidden. Work hand-stitched buttonholes on very delicate sheers, or make narrow tubing loops, or thread loops (several strands of thread covered with close blanket stitch). Choose small, light buttons and featherweight nylon zippers.

Hems
Hems should be either very narrow or very deep. Narrow hems may be hand-rolled or edge-stitched twice by machine. Deep double-turned hems can be attractive on sheers, and make the garment hang well. They can only be used on a straight edge.

Pressing
Make sure your iron and ironing board are both clean and smooth. Use a thin cotton or muslin press cloth and avoid using moisture on silky sheers. Always test for the best iron temperature and pressing method on a scrap of the fabric.

When working with lace, place the pattern pieces under the top layer so you can see where the motifs appear and arrange them effectively.

Vinyl fabrics

Vinyl is a kind of plastic and is available in several weights and textures, suitable for upholstery and household accessories as well as for garments. Most vinyl used in dressmaking has a nylon mesh backing. It comes in solid colors and also in prints. As it is waterproof and can be wiped clean, vinyl is well-suited to some children's clothing, such as raincoats and smocks for painting and other messy activities. The stiffer types of vinyl are best restricted to tote bags, aprons, placemats and tablecloths.

Vinyl requires special sewing techniques. The main thing to remember is that it is permanently marked by needles and pins, so the usual pinning and basting methods are inappropriate; and once it has been stitched, a seam or hem cannot be unpicked.

Choosing a pattern
When making a coat or jacket from vinyl, keep to a simple, straight, unbelted style with few seams and darts. Select raglan rather than set-in sleeves, as vinyl cannot be eased into the armhole. Avoid too many buttonholes, pressed pleats and gathers, unless the fabric is supple. If possible, use a pattern that you know will fit well to avoid alterations during assembling.

Cutting out
Open the fabric to its full width, place shiny side down and arrange the pattern pieces on the wrong side of the single layer. Avoid pinning, as it will mark the fabric. Instead, weight the pattern pieces down and draw around the edge of the pieces with chalk pencil.

Where you need to cut two pieces of a particular pattern piece, mark around the edge of the pattern, turn the tissue over and mark again for the second piece. Where pieces have to be cut on the fold, cut out the pattern in paper with the fold edge of the pattern on the fold of the paper to make the whole pattern. Mark the outline on single fabric.

Cut out using sharp dressmaking shears. Transfer all the necessary pattern markings to the fabric with chalk. If chalk does not show up clearly, use a soft pencil instead.

Stitching
Wherever possible, do not pin or baste. Hold edges together with paper clips or tape. Sometimes basting is unavoidable – for example, when inserting a zipper into a seam, when basting is the most effective way of holding the zipper in place before stitching.

Test stitch a sample of the fabric before stitching the garment, using polyester thread, a medium-size needle (14) and a medium/long stitch (8-12 per inch). A wedge-point needle should be used if the vinyl is not backed. If available, a needle made for synthetics is useful. Too many small stitches will weaken the seam. If necessary, slacken top tension slightly.

Use plain seams, stitched right sides together, and pink the edges for neatness. Clip into seam allowances on curves.

Pressing
Use the iron sparingly, and with extreme care. Never let the heated iron touch the right side of the fabric, as it

will melt the vinyl, which will then stick to the sole of the iron. Keep the temperature low, on the synthetics setting, and always cover the work with a press cloth.

Plain seams can normally be finger pressed open, but if they refuse to lie flat, the seam allowance can be glued in place with fabric glue, or both edges can be turned to one side and then stitched flat in a welt seam.

Topstitching
As the outer, double edges of vinyl items tend to "balloon" and cannot easily be pressed flat, they often look neater when topstitched. As this means stitching on the right side of the fabric, the presser foot may be inclined to stick. Try using a roller foot, which is specifically designed for sewing vinyl fabrics, or sprinkle the shiny surface with a little talcum powder. Stitching through tissue paper also helps to prevent the foot from sticking.

Hems
Make narrow, machine-stitched hems, or if the fabric can be glued successfully, secure in place with fabric glue.

Interfacing
Collars, cuffs, necklines and front edges can be interfaced for strength. Test iron-on interfacing on a scrap of vinyl fabric before using on the garment itself. The amount of heat needed to fuse it may impair the vinyl surface. If this is the case, use sew-in interfacing.

Fastenings
Machine-stitched buttonholes can be made on opaque vinyl fabrics, but test stitch first, using firm interfacing between the fabric layers to prevent stretching and a slightly larger, more open zigzag than usual. Reinforce buttons with shirt buttons on the back. Alternative fastenings are no-sew snaps and nylon tape. Zippers are inserted in the usual way, but with fabric glue stick used to hold the zipper in place before stitching.

Non-backed vinyl
Some types of vinyl are made without a backing. These range from the transparent and translucent kinds used for shower curtains to opaque, rubbery forms suitable for upholstery. Stitching techniques are similar to those for backed vinyl; however, a wedge-point needle should always be used. Do not press. This type of vinyl cannot usually be glued successfully, so topstitch the seam allowances to hold them in place.

Cutting out

Cut pattern pieces from single layer fabric. Weight down the tissue rather than pinning, draw around the edge with a chalk pencil and then cut out. Reverse the pattern before cutting the second piece of a pair.

Stitching a plain seam

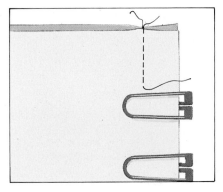

Place two layers of vinyl fabric right sides together, with raw edges even. Hold in position with paper clips along the edge to be stitched. Stitch the seam, removing the paper clips one by one as you reach them.

Pressing a seam

Plain seams can usually be finger pressed open. Flatten the seam further by running your fingernail firmly along the opened stitching line. Alternatively, press open, covering the work with a press cloth.

Welt seam

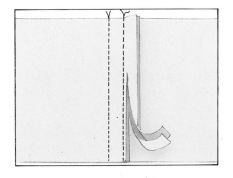

After stitching the seam, press both seam allowances to one side and stitch them flat through all layers, about ¼in from the seamline. Trim seam close to second row of stitching.

Topstitching

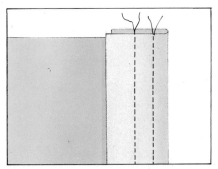

For easier topstitching on vinyl fabrics, place tissue paper underneath and on top of the fabric, and stitch through all thicknesses. Tear away the paper gently after stitching.

Hems

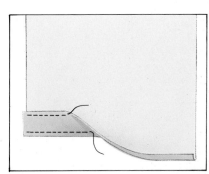

Trim the hemline evenly, allowing ⅝in hem allowance. Turn ¼in, then ⅜in, to wrong side and stitch in place along inner and outer edges to make a narrow machine-stitched hem.

Stripes, checks and plaids

Stripes, checks and plaids vary greatly in size and design. Small balanced designs are easiest to work with, although even these look better when matched correctly at seamlines. Larger designs take more planning but can be extremely effective when used imaginatively.

When choosing a pattern, look for designs with few seamlines and darts to cut across the fabric design. Avoid center front and back seams unless required for special effect. Yokes, cuffs, collars and pockets can form attractive contrasting features with plaids cut on the bias, or stripes running in contrasting direction. Avoid raglan sleeves, where the varying angles of the seamlines often make matching difficult.

Extra fabric is usually required for matching. On horizontal stripes and on plaids allow one fabric repeat for each main piece, though this does vary according to layout. Vertical stripes are best assessed individually.

Horizontal stripes
Horizontal or widthwise stripes run across the fabric from selvage to selvage, and are usually cut to run across a garment. Balanced stripes are the simplest and easiest to match. Unbalanced horizontal stripes have a one-way design and must be cut following a "with nap" layout so that the stripe sequence runs in the same order down each piece.

Matching horizontal stripes
Stripes should be matched at center front and back seams and side seams below bust dart. Stripes at sleeve caps should be matched to front armholes at and immediately above notch level.

Vertical stripes
Vertical or lengthwise stripes run along the length of the fabric parallel to the selvages and are usually cut with stripes running down the garment. Like horizontal stripes, vertical stripes may be balanced or unbalanced, but neither requires a "with nap" layout.

Unbalanced vertical stripes are in general cut with the stripe sequence running in one direction around the garment. A fabric layout with fabric folded in half lengthwise (selvages together at one side) will normally produce this result, though one should always check. Some designs, such as those with sloping center seams, look best with stripes matching in a chevron effect at center seam. With unbalanced stripes this is only possible if the sequence of stripes goes in opposite directions from the center outward. A layout with fabric folded in half widthwise (selvages together at both sides) will normally produce this result.

Matching vertical stripes
Where possible match stripe sequence in correct order across lengthwise

Balanced and unbalanced stripes

Balanced stripes are symmetrically spaced, sized and colored so the stripe sequence is the same in either direction from the center outward. Unbalanced stripes have the stripe sequence running in one direction only.

Unbalanced vertical stripes

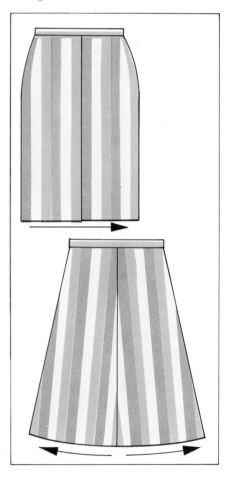

Unbalanced vertical stripes are usually arranged with the sequence of stripes running in one direction right around the garment (top). However garments with sloping center seams must have the stripe sequence reversing from center outward in order to match (above).

seams, and arrange stripes to meet in chevron formation on sloping seams. On bold stripes match similar stripes at shoulders where an exact match is not possible. It is often impossible to match stripes at both shoulder seams and side seams, or both at the center and side seams. In this case match whichever will be more visible. For example, on a blouse the shoulder seam and front opening are more visible than the side seam, which is concealed under the arm; whereas on a dress the side seam is more noticeable than the shoulder.

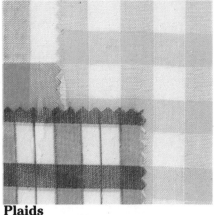

Plaids
Plaids, like stripes, may be balanced or unbalanced. A balanced plaid or a check is easiest to work with and may be regarded as a combination of balanced vertical and horizontal stripes; it is matched as for both types of stripe.

A completely unbalanced plaid is unbalanced on both the vertical and horizontal stripes—that is a one-way

design both widthwise and lengthwise. These need to be matched in correct sequence both lengthwise and widthwise. They are the most complicated of all types of plaid and are best avoided by the less experienced dressmaker.

Unbalanced plaids may also be a combination of balanced in one direction and unbalanced in the other. Again, these should be matched as for the appropriate combination of stripes.

Cutting out
First look at the fabric from a little distance, note the prominent lines of the design and decide where these will look best positioned on the garment. Simpler plaids and stripes may be cut through a double thickness of fabric, but make sure the underlayer is lined up accurately. More complex unbalanced designs are best cut through a single layer to ensure accurate matching. Remember to turn the pattern over when cutting a second piece to form a pair of pieces where required.

Line up pieces using notches as a guide to match at the required places. On complex fabrics trace the fabric repeat onto front pattern at matching points. Transfer tracing to the pattern pieces it must match with, then position second piece so tracing on the pattern matches appropriate repeat on fabric. Pieces must match at seamline rather than cutting line. On overlapping openings vertical stripes should continue in sequence across the finished opening.

Matching unbalanced checks

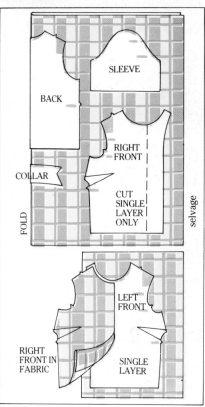

Match horizontally at side of front and back, and similar vertical stripes at shoulder. Match front sleeve notch horizontally to front armhole notch. Cut right front through a single layer. Turn pattern over and position left front to match right front with finished opening overlap matching.

Matching horizontal stripes

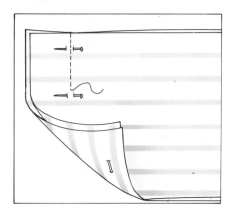

Machine stitching often pushes one layer of fabric along slightly, causing stripes to mis-match. Prevent this by pinning horizontally exactly on line of one stripe, making sure underlayer matches. Pin about 1½in apart, closer on difficult fabrics. Stitch slowly over pins.

Basting horizontal stripes

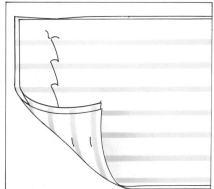

On difficult fabric straight basting may not hold stripes in line. Instead, baste by working a backstitch across seamline exactly on line of a stripe, making sure the underlayer matches. Then stitch diagonally downward to next stitch on next stripe.

Matching vertical stripes

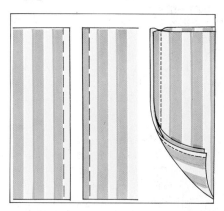

On straight seams match stripes to maintain stripe sequence. Match stripes at seamlines, not cut edges. Position the stitching line at the edge of a stripe where it will be less noticeable than part-way across the stripe.

Index